FINDING BALANCE

FINDING BALANCE

A FAMILY'S JOURNEY TO TREATMENT FOR BIPOLAR DISORDER

THE ORP LIBRARY

WRITTEN BY

JEFF KRUKAR, PH.D.

KATIE GUTIERREZ

WITH

NICOLETTE WEISENSEL, M.D.

JAMES G. BALESTRIERI

rtc
Publishing

rtc
Publishing

WRITERS OF THE ROUND TABLE PRESS
PO BOX 511
HIGHLAND PARK, IL 60035

Publisher	COREY MICHAEL BLAKE
Executive Editor	KATIE GUTIERREZ
Lead Writer	CHELSEA MCCUTCHIN
Director of Operations	KRISTIN WESTBERG
Facts Keeper	MIKE WINICOUR
Cover Design	ANALEE PAZ
Interior Design and Layout	SUNNY DIMARTINO
Proofreading	JONATHAN HIERHOLZER
Last Looks	CHRISTIAN PANNECK
Digital Book Conversion	SUNNY DIMARTINO
Digital Publishing	SUNNY DIMARTINO

Printed in the United States of America
First Edition: October 2015
10 9 8 7 6 5 4 3 2

Library of Congress Cataloging-in-Publication Data
Krukar, Jeff
Finding balance: a family's journey to treatment for bipolar disorder /
Jeff Krukar and Katie Gutierrez
with Nicolette Weisensel and James G. Balestrieri.—1st ed. p. cm.
Print ISBN: 978-1-939418-76-0   Digital ISBN: 978-1-939418-77-7
Library of Congress Control Number: 2015955325
Number 13 in the series: The ORP Library
The ORP Library: Finding Balance

RTC Publishing is an imprint of Writers of the Round Table, Inc.
Writers of the Round Table Press and the RTC Publishing logo
are trademarks of Writers of the Round Table, Inc.

CONTENTS

INTRODUCTION

Today, according to the U.S. Department of Health and Human Services, more than 5.5 million children—or eight percent of kids—in the U.S. have some form of disability. Whether the problem is physical, behavioral, or emotional, these children struggle to communicate, learn, and relate to others. While there is no longer *segregation* in the same sense as there was in the 1950s, what remains the same is the struggle. Even with all of our resources and technology, parents of children with disabilities fight battles every day to find the help and education their children need.

I have led Oconomowoc Residential Programs (ORP) for over thirty years. We're a family of companies offering specialized services and care for children, adolescents, and adults with disabilities. Too often, when parents of children with disabilities try to find funding for programs like ours, they are bombarded by red tape, conflicting information, or no information at all, so they struggle blindly for years to secure an appropriate education. Meanwhile, home life, and the child's wellbeing, suffers. In cases when parents and caretakers have exhausted their options—and their hope—ORP is here to help. We felt it was time to offer parents a new, unexpected tool to fight back: stories that educate, empower, and inspire.

The original idea was to create a library of comic books that could empower families with information to reclaim their rights. We wanted to give parents and caretakers the information they need to advocate for themselves, as well as provide educators and therapists with a therapeutic tool. And, of course, we wanted to reach the children—to offer them a visual representation of their journey that would show that they aren't alone, nor are they wrong or "bad" for their differences. What we found in the process of writing original stories for the comics is that these journeys are too long, too complex, to be contained within a standard comic. So what we are now creating is an ORP library of disabilities books—traditional books geared toward parents, caretakers, educators, and therapists, *and* comic books portraying the world through the eyes of children with disabilities. Both styles of books share what we have learned while advocating for families over the years while also honestly highlighting their emotional journeys. We're creating communication devices that anyone can read to understand complex disabilities in a new way.

In an ideal situation, these books will be used therapeutically, to communicate the message, and to help support the work ORP and companies like ours are doing. The industry has changed dramatically and is not likely to turn around any time soon—certainly not without more people being aware of families' struggles. We have an opportunity to put a face to the conversation, reach out to families, and start that dialogue.

Caring for children with disabilities consumes your life. We know that. And we want you to realize, through these stories, that you are not alone. We can help.

Sincerely,
Jim Balestrieri
CEO, Oconomowoc Residential Programs
www.orplibrary.com

A NOTE ABOUT THIS BOOK

Psychotropic medications are prescribed for the treatment of psychiatric disorders and specifically to improve a patient's emotional and behavioral health. In children and adolescents, just as in adults, lack of appropriate treatment can result in both short-term and long-term consequences.

Since the mid to late 1990s, there has been a significant increase in the understanding of childhood psychiatric disorders and a developing evidence base to support psychotropic medication and other nonmedication treatments for children with these disorders. Unfortunately, despite these advances, the majority of children and adolescents do not receive appropriate evaluations and treatment.

Changes in the U.S. mental health system over the last 20 years have resulted in a shortage of child and adolescent psychiatrists, increasingly limited insurance coverage for inpatient and residential treatment, and limited outpatient alternatives to support what many believe is an increased need for services. The front lines of the mental health services battle now squarely reside in the office of the primary care provider. These physicians now furnish over half of the mental health treatment in the U.S. and are believed to prescribe the majority of psychotropic medications used by children and adolescents (Bazelton Center). While each primary care provider's education and experience varies, most are unlikely to have the appropriate resources to treat youth who have a complicated set of challenges.

Unfortunately, there has also been an insufficient number of psychotropic medication trials with children and adolescents. This has left few psychotropic medications that are Food and Drug Administration (FDA) approved for use in youth. As a result, many psychotropic medications prescribed for this age group are administered "off label"—that is, not FDA approved for use in children and adolescences for certain disorders or age ranges. In clinical practice, however, the majority of "off label" psychotropic medications do appear to be beneficial and safe in youth.

Psychotropic medications are only one component of a comprehensive biopsychosocial treatment plan, which must be a collaborative team effort and include other components in addition to medication. The term *biopsychosocial* recognizes the three domains that impact a youth's emotional and behavioral well-being:

1. *Bio* refers to "biological," and includes physical health and genetic factors. Psychotropic medications affect biological factors by altering the levels of chemicals in the brain that help to regulate the activity of neurons (brain cells) that determine emotions, mood, and behavior.

2. *Psycho* refers to psychological factors in the youth that contribute to emotional and behavioral functioning, including feelings and thoughts, goals, and understanding of self and environment.

3. *Social* refers to the environmental factors that influence a youth's functioning, such as family circumstances and relationships and other resources in the community, including those provided by human service agencies and natural supports. Within the social domain, it is particularly important to obtain the evaluation of history of trauma and disrupted attachments.

Health professionals, families, advocates, and human service providers must carefully assess the risks and benefits of using psychotropic medications in children and adolescents. Readers are encouraged to educate themselves appropriately depending on their individual situation, and to be careful to obtain information from reputable sources. An appendix is located at the end of this book with resources to consider using.

The young man depicted in the following story struggles with significant emotional and behavioral difficulties. You may note similarities to your own experiences or those of a loved one, student, or patient. If so, this book is meant to provide a roadmap, of sorts. It is our hope that the education it provides will help you navigate the complex journey experienced by those whose worlds intersect with the use of psychotropic medications.

Jim Balestrieri
CEO, Oconomowoc Residential Programs

CHAPTER 1

What's the point of carding people when everyone fakes it? As Alex Magana hands over the ID claiming he's twenty-two, it all seems like a tacit agreement created to allow everyone to do what they're going to do anyway, guilt-free. Take this lady behind the counter of Mel's Liquors: gray hair escaping her bun in wild frizz, toad-brown eyes swollen behind smudged glasses, overweight and barely fitting into the constraints of her chair—but with a nice smile, a kind one, Alex acknowledges. Well, later, if anyone asks her about him, she can say she carded him; of course she did. She does her job, she doesn't ever sell to kids—why would she risk her hide for them? And technically, she'd be telling the truth.

"Thank you," Alex says, taking the paper bag she proffers. He can almost taste the harshness of the Old Crow, the bitter heat as it snakes into his chest, lighting him up, setting him on fire. "Oh, wait," he says. He grabs three mini-bottles of Scotch, and grins. "You never know when these might come in handy."

"You just be careful out there," the woman says, shaking her head but smiling a little. She probably has sons, maybe grandsons by now. Alex can't tell how old she

1

is. She rings him up, takes his last seven dollars, and passes the minis back to him.

Alex drives around the corner to a Walmart parking lot before opening the Old Crow. It's only one p.m., but the swirling snow and low gray clouds make it look much later. Alex turns up the radio volume until he feels the bass in his chest, as if it's a defibrillator, starting his heart. That's what he needs. That's exactly what he needs. He takes a long pull of the Old Crow, eyes immediately smarting. "Yeeeeooow!" he howls, hardly audible over the music, and laughs, taking another swig. This is it; this is what he's been after, just a little warmth, a little jumpstart to get him out of this funk. And what's wrong with that? But to his mom, booze is the devil. Well, the devil and an angel at once, tempting her from all directions, and she can't have it, she says. Can't have any of this shit in the house. She threw a fit last time she found the empties in his room, bursting into angry tears, asking if he really wants her to send him to rehab, because she will, she threatens. She'll do it.

Supposedly he's depressed. That's what the doctor says, but the doctor in question is Alex's pediatrician. Grandma-types who give lollipops to kids shouldn't be allowed to prescribe antidepressants for grown men, Alex thinks, becoming more and more convinced as his mood rises that he's not depressed. Jesus! It's just the long winter months. Soon as he turns eighteen in June, he's leaving this miserable place. Screw his last year of high school. He'd be done by then anyway if he hadn't been held back. Bastards. He's going to move down somewhere warm, Florida, maybe—but Miami, where the hot chicks are, not where all the old fogeys like his grandparents live, in Fort Lauderdale or wherever. He'll get a job at a bar; he'll be *banking* on tips, especially from the spring break crowd, all those wild girls screaming and eager to show their bodies and leave money behind. He'll be drunk all the time, because that's when he feels the best, most like himself, or like he remembers himself feeling once.

Alex's phone is vibrating in the console. His mom. Of course. What did he say he was leaving the house for? To pick up lunch or something? He can't remember. It doesn't matter. What *matters* is that he's finally feeling better. There's a laugh, tight in his throat, and he's awake and alert but with a heaviness behind his eyeballs that tells him maybe, maybe he'll be able to sleep later. When was the last time he slept? Lately, nights have been solely for chatting online, blowing smoke out his bedroom window.

He ignores his mom's call. Instead, he scrolls through his texts until he gets to Bettany. God, she's hot, with her ripped black jeans and Sanskrit tattoo on her right wrist, right over her racing pulse. *Hey*, he types, *wanna party?*

The ellipses pop up, indicating she's writing back, and then disappear. He raises the bottle to his mouth again, eyes never leaving the screen. The ellipses return, followed by *Lol what like right now?*

Yeah. Cmon it'll be fun. He switches over to Snapchat and takes a quick scrolling video of the booze, ending on his face, winking. Send. He waits.

Ur crazy! Lolol.

So?

Come pick me up. Text when ur outside.

C u soon, he writes.

. . .

Jennifer Magana stared at the backseat of her son's car. She'd had a suspicion, a hollowness in her belly, that Alex was returning to his wild ways, but she had hoped her spontaneous search would prove her wrong. Now she gaped at not only the fast food wrappers and soggy-bottomed soda cups she'd expect in a seventeen-year-old boy's domain, but also empty boxes of cigarettes, empty mini-bottles of Scotch, an upended whiskey bottle, and several condoms, discarded from their wrappers. The mess lay in plain sight on the floorboard of the second-hand sedan that Jennifer had worked overtime for six months to afford. The whole car stank.

Jennifer sank to the curb, her throat tight. The cold cement instantly seeped through her jeans, chilling her. She felt sick. She remembered when her own car looked like this (minus the condoms), a veritable graveyard of vodka bottles that, later, in a haze of shame and disbelief, she'd swear weren't hers. How could she possibly drink so much vodka? Her then-husband, Sebastian, would look at her in disgust, and all she'd be thinking about was how she wished there was a little more left in one of those bottles that couldn't possibly be hers. Now Alex . . .

She hauled herself from the ground. One part of her—the mother who was still instinctively drawn to clean up after her son—wanted to grab a trash bag from inside the house and sweep all of this mess from the car so they could pretend it didn't exist; so she could save Alex from the shame. Another part of her—the mother who was used to being the disciplinarian, who believed there should be consequences for one's actions—wanted to drag the sleeping Alex out here to confront the physical evidence of his behavior. And a third part of her—the recovering alcoholic—wanted to hug her son, to apologize, to tell him it was one day at a time, always.

But *was* Alex a burgeoning alcoholic? Just because she had been, at that age, didn't mean he was following that worn tread. It was possible it was something else—that he was acting out. He was a teenaged boy, for God's sake. She thought back to the seventeen-year-olds of her youth, joints dangling from their lips, beer cans winking in the moonlight. They were just having fun. Most of them, anyway.

Shaking slightly with cold, Jennifer locked Alex's car and trudged inside the house. She needed to call Sebastian. First, she made a pot of coffee. Even now, her hands ached for a glass to hold during stressful conversations.

"Hey." Sebastian answered on the fourth ring, right as Jennifer was preparing her voicemail. He sounded harried, as though she were interrupting him from something important. Sebastian always had a way of making her feel like an inconvenience. "What's going on?"

Jennifer paced the length of her small kitchen, touching the wall like a relay runner before turning and pacing in the opposite direction. She tucked her short brown hair behind her ears. "I just found condoms, beer bottles, and empty packs of cigarettes in Alex's car."

Sebastian was silent for a moment. Then he said, "Well, he is seventeen. What do you expect?"

The blood rushed from Jennifer's neck to her hairline. She made herself count to three, the way their VA family therapist had suggested once upon a time, before responding. "I expect for his father to give more of a damn," she said. (Well, that count didn't work.) "What if he crashes his car and kills someone? Kills himself? Or gets someone pregnant? How do you think we would deal with any of that?" A heat was rising in her chest that she just couldn't release. She sat down and held her coffee cup tightly with one hand.

"You're exaggerating," Sebastian said, and Jennifer could hear a woman's voice—*that* woman's voice—speaking to Sebastian in the background. "Look, I have to go. I'll talk to him later, okay? Would that make you happy?"

Jennifer squeezed her eyes shut to fight the sudden sting. Would that make her happy? No. It would have made her happy if the man she'd married at twenty-one were still interested in being her husband and the father of their son, instead of father to a toddler whose mother was barely out of her teens herself. "Fine," she said. "Thanks."

Jennifer dropped her phone and stared into the blackness of her coffee. The call had brought no comfort, no sense that she wasn't in this alone.

Alex had pulled away so much in the past year, but she had told herself that no news—no administrative phone calls from school, no angry parents knocking at her door, no police—meant that he was doing better. Now she knew: her hope served as blinders.

Alex had always been different from other kids. As far back as preschool, he was his own little person. Once, the teacher was lining the kids up to go outside for their afternoon recess. The children were all excited to get onto the playground, but none so much as Alex. He pulled out of the line and started to dance, alone. He took off his shirt, thrashing his arms to an imaginary band, and then stripped off his pants. The other kids had laughed, pointing, which had enraged Alex so much that he struck one little boy across the face. Of course, the teacher called Jennifer right away, and Jennifer was infuriated by the smug look of disapproval on the teacher's face; they could barely afford this school. Jennifer was just twenty-six then and never got enough sleep between working two jobs and taking care of Alex, and instead of talking to him calmly about appropriate behavior, she'd yelled at him on their way home. "You don't hit!" she'd said, taking hold of his shoulder to make sure he was paying attention. "Do you understand me?" With brown eyes filling with tears, Alex simply nodded.

But when Alex was in elementary school, Jennifer was called in at least once a week because he was fighting or being a distraction in class. (And why didn't they ever call Sebastian? she thought now, bitterly. It was always moms who got the thankless work, while dads got to swoop in with godlike randomness, dangling afternoons fishing and other treasured "guy time" as a replacement for regular time not spent together.) Jennifer had become the parent who stretched her mouth into thin smiles at PTA events. She was the one who had explained to Alex that no one had come to his birthday party because people went on vacations over the summer, and that he was never invited for a second sleepover because maybe the other child's parents liked to have privacy.

She looked at the oven clock. Alex should be downstairs any minute for breakfast, but Jennifer hadn't heard him rustling around upstairs. Her heart beat in her throat as she headed for the stairs. Confrontations with Alex never ended well, but they needed to happen. He couldn't have two parents who minimized his behavior.

"Alex!" Jennifer said, more forcefully than she felt,

7

from outside her son's door. "What are you doing in there?"

No response. She shifted her weight from one foot to the other. "Alex! It's time to get up. You have to leave for school in fifteen minutes, and I need to talk to you about something."

"I'm sick, Mom," Alex called back, his voice raspy with sleep.

Jennifer pushed his door open. Alex's sheets made a tangled cocoon around him, only the top of his curly hair visible over the comforter.

"Of course you're sick. Booze and cigarettes will do that to you," Jennifer said sharply. "I found your trash in your car."

Alex poked his head out from the covers. "None of that stuff is even mine," he said. "You're just making stupid assumptions." He pulled the quilt over his head again. "Get out of here before you piss me off. I don't feel well, I'm not coming out, and I'm not talking about this anymore. Besides," he added, lowering the quilt to glare at Jennifer with new fire, "what the hell were you even doing in my car? Spying on me? What I do is my own damn business."

"I thought none of it was yours," Jennifer said, raising her eyebrows. Alex didn't respond, and she marched to her son's bed and pulled the quilt off him. "And it's not your own damn business. Until you're eighteen and out of this house, paying your own bills, what you do is *my* damn business. I haven't worked as hard as I have to see you ruin your life before you're even twenty-one."

"What, like you getting knocked up?" Alex retorted. "Sorry to have shit on your grand plans. Which were what, anyway?"

Jennifer was both stricken and livid. "That's not what I meant."

"Right." Alex turned away from her, curling into a ball. He pulled a pillow over his head. "Mom, seriously, get the hell out. I'm tired." After a beat, he added, "I only did it so I could sleep."

"What?" Jennifer's arms were crossed against her chest as she stared down at her son. "What are you talking about?"

"See, you don't even know! You have no fucking idea that I haven't slept in like a week. Do you know what that feels like?" When he turned back to her, his eyes glinted with tears. Beneath them, gray half-moons gave his unshaven face a haggard appearance, as if he were much older than seventeen.

Jennifer sat down on the edge of his bed. "What do you mean you haven't slept in a week? That's impossible. You—"

"Don't tell me what's impossible!" Alex was yelling, scrambling to his feet, and Jennifer launched to hers, startled. "You have no idea what I'm going through! So *what* if I drink a little if it actually lets me get some goddamn *rest*!"

"Okay." Jennifer held up her hands, palms out. Alex was a full foot taller than she was, still bony but strong, and as he took a step toward her, her heart rate spiked. "Why don't you tell me? Tell me what you've been going through."

Alex was breathing hard. A vein in his neck was throbbing, and in that moment, any response seemed possible. Finally, he bumped her away with his shoulder as he walked toward the door.

"We're done here," he said.

"Turn around."

He did, slowly; his jaw clenched.

"You may be seventeen," Jennifer said, "but I'm still your mother, and you will be respectful of me. You will clean your car and come straight home after school, from now until I say otherwise. What if something happened, Alex? Do you ever, even once, think of the consequences of your actions?"

The air in the room stilled. With a kind of roar, Alex grabbed his chemistry textbook from his desk and hurled it against the wall before striding to Jennifer and yelling right down in her face.

"I don't care what you think, I don't care about consequences, I don't care about anything, so just BACK! OFF!" His voice grew louder and louder, and Jennifer felt a quiet crumple in her heart that this was her son, her baby, screaming at her as if he hated her.

Alex stormed from the room, and Jennifer slipped out after him, slinking back to her room like an injured cat.

• • •

Everyone described Alex as a troubled young man. Two years ago, when he was fifteen, he could go from delightfully charming one day to frighteningly temperamental the next. She and Sebastian were in the middle of their divorce, and Jennifer told herself that Alex was just reacting to the change. He was angry. Hell, she was angry too, drinking what she knew to be too many vodka tonics too early in the day. Years earlier, when Alex was too young to remember, she'd gone through therapy to help her manage her addiction. It had saved her life. But when that life seemed to be collapsing, the lure of something to dull the pain was too strong to ignore. So she'd made excuses for herself and excuses for Alex, even when she received the worst call yet from his assistant principal.

"Mrs. Magana?" Mr. Phelps's voice was cold.

"Yes, Mr. Phelps." Jennifer knew his tone well. She'd been in touch with him no fewer than thirty times over the past two years.

"I have Alex in my office. He's being detained by our school resource officer." There was a hint of amusement in his voice, as if he were excited that things had escalated to the point of calling in the police.

"What? What happened?"

"Alex refused to tuck in his shirt. I saw him in the lunch line and informed him that he was violating dress code, and he got mouthy with me. When I asked him to come back to my office, he told me, in the presence of many witnesses—both teachers and students—that if he came back to my office, he would kill me in it."

Jennifer's stomach lurched. "Mr. Phelps, I'm so sorry. Alex just gets—"

"Mrs. Magana, we have to take threats very seriously," Mr. Phelps interrupted. "Alex will be suspended for five days. We'd also like to schedule a district office meeting with the superintendent to discuss Alex's future here. You'll need to come get him right now and sign the paperwork in my office indicating that you are in agreement." Mr. Phelps was matter of fact, stony. Jennifer glanced at the freezer, where she knew a bottle of vodka was tucked, frosting so purely. Just one sip wouldn't hurt before she went to pick up Alex.

One sip turned into a stiff drink, several fingers of

vodka on ice, and then another, and then Jennifer forced herself to replace the bottle and drive to the school. By the time she got there, she had arrived at a conclusion: sooner or later, Alex would be expelled. He would have that on his record. It would be smarter, better for him, to pull him out now and enroll him somewhere else. When Jennifer drank, she made swift decisions, most often without consulting Sebastian. She could weather whatever temper tantrum Sebastian threw, she told herself. She was doing what was best for her son.

The next week, she and Sebastian—who was still furious—enrolled Alex in McNeal, an alternative school for students with significant behavioral problems and trouble with authority. Alex had repeated freshman year at his previous school because of poor grades and not completing homework, but Jennifer hoped that once he acclimated as a sophomore at McNeal, he would do okay. While he still acted out, the tough approach that the teachers took didn't require a daily phone call to Jennifer—only three or four per month. With the divorce finalized, Sebastian living with his nubile new girlfriend, and Alex's behavior seemingly more stable, Jennifer had found a kernel of strength and called her old therapist, who immediately scheduled an appointment. Everything seemed, if not great, at least better—until now. What Jennifer had found in Alex's car, their heated confrontation . . . this only cemented the unspoken worry Jennifer had felt for months. Some days, he said he hated himself, crying in Jennifer's lap, and other days—like today—he reared up like a revolutionary. And on still other days, Alex was so revved up, so bursting with energy and drive and charisma, that Jennifer was both pleased and alarmed. Whatever Sebastian said, she knew this wasn't just "boys being boys."

Over the years, various teachers and guidance counselors had recommended that she and Sebastian get Alex evaluated for attention deficit hyperactivity disorder or oppositional defiant disorder, but Jennifer had never shared those ideas with her husband, knowing he would only get irritated and defensive. She was irritated and defensive too, if she was being honest. Who were these people to suggest something was wrong with her son? She'd always looked at her own family as proof: five kids, four of them boys, all of them rambunctious and opinionated and rebellious. But one of her brothers was a lawyer, one owned his own automotive repair shop, one was in construction, and one did . . . well, he did a lot of things; mostly he traveled, making money as he went. They weren't perfect men, by any means, but they were surviving, providing for their families. So surely Alex would grow out of his "quirks," as she used to call them. At least, this was her reasoning when he was younger.

> *Attention deficit hyperactivity disorder* (ADHD) is one of the most common childhood disorders and can continue through adolescence and adulthood. Symptoms include difficulty staying focused and paying attention, difficulty controlling behavior, and hyperactivity (overactivity).

> *Oppositional defiant disorder* is characterized by an ongoing pattern of uncooperative, defiant, and hostile behavior toward authority figures that seriously interferes with the child or adolescent's day-to-day functioning.

But an erratic teenager with a bellowing voice who towered over her was more unsettling. This year, Jennifer felt sure that Alex was struggling with depression. His moodiness just didn't seem like normal teenaged moodiness.

It had a weight to it, a heft. On Alex's sad days, he wasn't just sad; he was *hopeless*. He told her once, in tears, "It's like, I know winter ends, right? It always has, even if sometimes it takes longer. In my *head*, I know that. But the way I feel right now, it's like I can't convince myself that winter won't last forever." She'd sat next to him on his bed, his head on her shoulder, and wrapped her arms around him, aching for this boy who felt caught in endless winter.

That's why she'd made an appointment with his pediatrician. Dr. Alice Morgan had known Alex since he was a baby. Jennifer trusted her to take time with him, to be thoughtful in her approach. She'd given Alex a checkup and spent some time with him alone, talking, before asking Jennifer to come back into the room.

"Physically," she said, "everything looks fine, save for Alex being a little underweight for his age. And I'm sure college will fix that." She smiled at him. "But from what Alex has told me about his moods, I'm worried that he's dealing with depression."

"That's exactly what I thought!" Jennifer burst out.

"You don't have to sound so happy about it," Alex muttered, staring at his lap.

Jennifer felt herself flush. "That's not what I meant," she started, but Dr. Morgan held up a hand.

"It's okay," she said. "I understand. Jennifer, I think our best course of action is to start Alex on an antidepressant. How would you feel about that?"

Antidepressant medication is a type of psychotropic medication used to treat depression. This medication may also be used to treat other mental disorders as deemed appropriate by a physician, including anxiety disorders, obsessive-compulsive disorder, and post-traumatic stress disorder.

Quietly, Jennifer said, "I was on them for a while, shortly after Alex was born."

Alex looked up, surprised. "You were?"

"I had postpartum depression," she said. "It was pretty severe." She shivered, remembering once sitting all day in the same rocking chair with Alex, not even changing him, because she was convinced that if she separated him from the safety of her body, he would die. "They really helped me, honey," she said.

Alex was the very image of morose: eyes swollen, cheeks sunken, curly hair a greasy mop on his head. Jennifer hated herself for taking so long to see it.

"Alex?" Dr. Morgan prompted. "How do you feel about trying antidepressants?"

"Crazy," he mumbled. Quickly, he swiped at his eyes.

"Honey, there's nothing crazy about you," Jennifer said. She wanted to go to him, but she knew he'd be embarrassed by her affection. "This is no different than treating any other kind of illness. You're not angry with yourself when you get strep throat, are you?"

Alex didn't answer for a moment. "It's not the same thing," he said finally. "This is my brain. You're telling me something's wrong with my *brain*," he said to Dr. Morgan.

"Alex," Dr. Morgan said, "did you know that more than one in ten adolescents struggle with a depressive disorder?[1] That means that—how many people are in each class of yours? Thirty?"

Alex nodded. "Around there."

---

1   Source: National Institute of Mental Health

Major depression has severe symptoms that interfere with one's ability to work, sleep, study, eat, and enjoy life. This is more than just feeling blue or down. Along with either a depressed mood or difficulty enjoying things, symptoms can include significant weight loss or weight gain, sleeping too much or trouble sleeping, slowed or sped-up movements, fatigue or loss of energy, feelings of worthlessness or inappropriate guilt, problems with concentration or making decisions, and recurrent thoughts of death or suicide.

"That means that there are probably three students in any given class you're in who are dealing with something similar to what you are. You're not alone, and you're not crazy. The neurotransmitters in your brain just need a little help."

Neurotransmitters are chemical messengers in the brain that allow for communication between neurons (cells in the brain). Mental illnesses, such as depression, can occur when this process does not work correctly.

Dr. Morgan was focused exclusively on Alex, giving her shoulder to Jennifer, and Jennifer was grateful. She knew from her struggle with addiction that the best chance of adherence came when change felt like one's own choice. If Alex was going to be faithful about taking his meds, he needed to feel that this was *his* decision.

"Fine," he said finally. "I mean, what do I have to lose?"

Secretly, Jennifer agreed. She half listened as Dr. Morgan discussed potential side effects: nausea; increased appetite and weight gain (which wouldn't be such a bad thing for Alex); fatigue or, conversely, insomnia; dry mouth; constipation . . . This seemed like the same list as on any number of medications. The worst Jennifer had experienced was loss of sexual desire, which, at least initially, she was able to chalk up to the trauma of child-birth and the depression itself; but after a year, when the depression had abated and her body had healed, and she still had no interest in sex with Sebastian, it occurred to her that it could be the medication. When she stopped taking it, her normal libido returned. Well, she thought, it wouldn't be such a bad thing if Alex lost some interest in sex, would it?

But now, only a week and a half since Alex had started the medication, he seemed to be getting *worse*, not better. There was a frenzied look in his eyes, a wildness, and not sleeping for a week? What was that about? Then there was the alcohol and—Jennifer cringed, thinking about the condoms—the sex. No, this wasn't good.

When the front door slammed downstairs, indicating that Alex had left for school, she called the pediatrician. It was time for a second visit.

CHAPTER 2

Alex doesn't intend to skip school, but when he approaches the gates, he keeps driving. And as soon as he does, it just feels right. What does he need school for, anyway? He's smarter, more creative, more innovative, than all those fuck-ups in there, every one of them bearing the label of "emotionally disturbed"—Alex included; only for him, it's not true. It's only that he's so far ahead of those his age that no one knows where to place him, what to call him. He could go in there and pass every test they give him, even next year's tests, and not just pass them but *ace* them. He's so sure of this that his chest balloons with pride. Maybe what he'll do is just ask to take the GED, finish up this charade a whole year and a half early and— no. Why even do that? What does he have to prove? No one who's ever been great has been great because they got their high school diploma. High school is irrelevant. It's babysitting, just a way to pass the time until a slew of eighteenth birthdays, when everyone—parents, kids, teachers—can be free. The truth is, this whole idea of eighteen signifying the age of adulthood is bullshit. Look at history. Hell, look at other places in the world *today*, and there's the proof that kids stop being kids long before eighteen, living and working and *contributing* to the world as young as eight, nine, ten. This whole eighteen thing is just another way for society to control people, to hold on to them just a little longer in hopes of indoctrinating them into the dominant ways of thinking. It's all just brainwashing. It's all bullshit. There needs to be a way to break out of it. There is a way, and it's tugging at Alex's brain, tickling it with light fingers, something about a documentary on Netflix . . . ?

Alex is in the fast lane, though he can't remember when he merged onto the highway. His mind is racing, each thought trampling the heels of the one before so that it seems that dozens of thought processes are happening simultaneously. At the same time he's thinking of society's command-and-control over adolescents and the reality that childhood is only a construct created to benefit *them*, he's also thinking about his father, for some reason, and he's angry. It's been two years, but he still remembers the day his parents sat him down in the living room and told him they would be divorcing, but they both still loved him and blah blah blah, straight out of the How to Break Divorce to Your Kids brochure. Alex could see right through them. True, he hadn't noticed before, but now he read the guilt in his dad's tired eyes as clearly as if he'd caught him in the act, and he read the shock and betrayal and grief in the twist of his mother's hands, and he could tell by the shaking of her fingers that she'd gone back to drinking, and, well, he couldn't blame her. His dad's girlfriend, Sherry, had skin so smooth she could pass for one of Alex's classmates, except she held herself so straight and tall and walked so confidently in those sexy heels that no way she was a teenager. College, maybe. He didn't know, not then.

He didn't want to know. And now, he grips the steering wheel harder, feeling the same sense of betrayal his mom must still feel at the thought of them together, with a son. Alex can't be replaced—he knows that, he's too special—but still, it stings. He's only met the kid two or three times—Sherry always seems to be out with him when Alex visits his father—and feels no connection to him. Alex isn't even sure he'd recognize the kid in a lineup. A baby lineup. The thought of it, a bunch of gurgling milk-spew babies all propped up against a wall, behind a two-way mirror, makes him laugh.

And while *these* thoughts are flitting through his mind, he's thinking of Bettany, of the last time they were together, how down she was to take shots of Old Crow and play a game of Strip Truth—answer a question or take off a layer of clothing—and even though she was bundled in hat and jacket and scarf and boots—those hot Timberland boots she pulls off—everything came off fast. It's all a blur to him, a dreamlike sequence of skin and warmth and ecstasy, and he wants it again. Now.

Alex looks at the clock and blinks. It's saying it's almost noon, but he passed his school just after eight. That was only a few minutes ago. Wasn't it? He grabs his phone from the passenger seat, stunned to see that it agrees with the car: it's almost noon. He's almost out of gas. Where the hell is he? For a second he feels dizzy, convinced that somehow both clocks have been changed, that someone is trying to trick him. Maybe his mom, teaching him a lesson. Only she couldn't have known he would skip school today; not even *he* knew that. Unless . . . Could she somehow know anyway, even before he did? He shakes off the thought, though it chills him.

He pulls over at the next gas station to fill up. With change from the last fifty in his possession, he buys a twelve-pack. He's got four hours to kill on the drive home, apparently; he may as well relax a little.

The temperature's dropped right off again; it's in the low twenties, and Alex forgot to grab a jacket before leaving the house. Though the hair is up on his arms as he pumps gas into his car, he's not cold. He feels . . . invigorated. Happy, even. He hikes the radio volume way up (has it really been *off* all this time?) and starts shouting along with Lil Wayne and Nicki Minaj. Damn, this is nice. This is a good day. This is what he misses by being in school; this is what they're trying to steal from him: life itself. The sweet swell of pleasure that comes just through the sheer act of breathing! Of accepting the oxygen the world offers and—

"Hey—hey! Kid!"

Alex looks over. A middle-aged black man is calling to him, pointing.

"Hey, your gas is going over! And you shouldn't have your car on. Turn your car off. Didn't anyone teach you how to fill up? You wanna ignite those fumes?"

Alex grins. He pulls a red plastic lighter from his pocket. "Hey, yourself. Why don't you mind your own business? Besides, if I wanted to start something, I'd just light this fucker up."

The man's face slackens. Quickly, he pulls the fuel nozzle from his Suburban and lodges it back in place. "Take it easy," he says, hurrying to his door. "I was just trying to help, all right?"

He drives off as Alex is still standing there, laughing, rubbing his thumb over the spark wheel.

...

The world is dark and quiet when Alex pulls into the driveway. Except for his house. Every light is on, blaring. It's like his house is screaming at the neighborhood, look at me, look at me, pay attention to ME! His dad's lame, baby-friendly CRV is parked out front. Why would his dad be here?

He's wobbly on his feet, laughing at his missteps. There's a buzzing inside his skin, an electric energy that makes him feel high. The first time he tries to slide the key in the lock, he misses entirely, scratching the wood beside it. The second time, the door flies open and he nearly falls into his mother's arms.

"Oh, thank God!" she exclaims, pulling him inside. "Alex, we've been so worried. Where have you been?"

She holds him by the elbows and looks at him, and as she does, her expression of relieved happiness changes. He watches in fascination. His mother's face is so pliable. She could be an actress. He reaches down and pinches one of her cheeks.

"Sebastian!" she yells.

His father emerges from the kitchen, telephone in hand. He hangs up when he sees Alex. "Jesus Christ, Alex," he snaps, but he looks relieved, too. "It's almost midnight. You nearly gave your mom a heart attack. The school called this morning and said you never showed up. I was this close to reporting you missing!"

"It would take you more than twelve hours to report me missing?" Alex asks, smirking. "Yeah, you must have been real worried." He leans back against the front door, crossing his arms to keep himself from swaying. The house is too bright. They're killing his trip. He just wants to get upstairs, have his last cigarette of the day, and pass out.

"You reek of booze," Alex's mother said. Her voice broke. "You've been *driving* like this? Alex—"

"Mom, stop, okay?" Irritation rises in Alex so quickly it takes his breath away. He pushes off the door and tries to move past her, but she grabs his wrist.

"No, not okay!" Her grip tightens. "This is *not* okay, do you understand me? You're going to come into the kitchen and answer our questions."

Alex scoffs. It's a joke, his five-foot-two mother trying to act tough while his father hangs quietly in the background. He wrenches his wrist away with ease. "Screw you."

"Alejandro!" his father bellows.

"Now we're Mexican," Alex snickers.

His father's face darkens with anger, and for a moment, Alex wonders: how far can he push? How close are they to breaking already, without him even trying? What would it take to make his father throw a fist or his mother slap him? He could claim abuse. Get emancipated. Finally be on his own, where he didn't have to answer to anyone.

"You see?" his mom said quietly to his dad. "You know what, Alex? Go upstairs. Go to bed. We'll talk about this in the morning."

Alex smiles at them, luminous, impervious. He makes sure to bump each of their shoulders on his way to the staircase. He wants them to know—*he's* the one in control.

. . .

Sebastian stayed for another half hour after Alex went upstairs. They sat in the living room, where Jennifer pulled a blanket over her lap on the leather couch and Sebastian sat adjacent to her in the matching, albeit much older, recliner.

"I think it's the meds," Jennifer said. "I really do. I was worried about him before, obviously, but his behavior these last couple of weeks has been totally different than it was when we first went to the pediatrician. It's night and day."

Sebastian shook his head. His graying dark hair was rumpled and long. His new wife must like it that way, Jennifer thought. He said, "I still can't believe you had him go on antidepressants without even telling me. What kind of crap is that, Jennifer?"

"The kind of crap that happens when you're so quick to dismiss everything he does as typical teenage angst," Jennifer snapped back. "Look, you haven't lived here in two years. He's never cried in your arms, telling you how worthless he feels and how he can't imagine ever feeling better. It's awful, Seba. And then this morning, throwing his book the way he did . . . I thought he actually might hit me. What am I supposed to do? I'm on my own now."

A lump had risen to Jennifer's throat, and she swallowed it back carefully, chipping it away.

"Alex inherited my father's temper," Sebastian said, not looking at her. He rarely spoke of his father, and typically only in reverent tones. Sebastian's father, Alejandro, had been a brilliant musician. He'd played any instrument he could get his hands on and was the life of the party. Two weeks before Sebastian and Jennifer's wedding, Sebastian's father had taken his own life. Sebastian's mother had left him six months earlier, after thirty years of cleaning up after his rock-and-roll parties and pulling him out of bed and into a cold shower so that he could make a gig and feed the family that night. "But Alex is going to be different," Sebastian added. "He's just going through a stage."

Jennifer sighed. She knew that Sebastian had just admitted his biggest fear—that his son and his father were linked through genetic destiny. That somehow he'd failed Alex as his father, in the same way Sebastian felt failed by his father. Sebastian had undergone extensive therapy, and while his therapist had affirmed that his father was, without a doubt, mentally ill, and there was nothing that Sebastian could have done for him, Sebastian had a blind spot when it came to his own son.

"You see?" she said. "This is what I'm talking about."

They were both quiet, and the room seemed too small suddenly, too tight and warm with its rust-red walls and two fake Persian rugs piled on top of each other. This was where they'd told Alex about their divorce. Alex had sat right where Sebastian sat now, looking between them with an unreadable expression. He hadn't said a word, just got up and went upstairs, closing the door to his room. Sebastian had risen immediately afterwards and left the house. Jennifer had remained sitting, her hands in her lap, unblinking, it seemed, for hours. Shock, she supposed. The startled anguish of losing something she'd once thought was permanent.

She broke the silence. "I've made a follow-up appointment with the pediatrician this week. I want to try him on a different medicine." Her tone was defiant. It didn't matter to her what Sebastian said; she knew this was the right thing to do.

He sighed as he stood from the recliner. Without meeting her eyes, he said, "Do what you have to do."

...

Three days passed quickly, the way they do when there is little slowing down and no stopping. Alex was raw energy, so inattentive and distractible in class that he'd been sent home twice for spontaneously jumping from his seat and pacing around the room, once even going to the front of the class and attempting to take over the science teacher's lecture. At home, doors were constantly slamming, not out of anger but from the strength of Alex's energy. He went on two-hour runs, coming home with his gray sweatshirt soaked in sweat. He talked so quickly that Jennifer constantly had to ask him to repeat himself, but when he did, it was no clearer. His cheeks were flushed, his eyes pink-rimmed and wild. The only positive thing, as far as Jennifer was concerned, was that he was eating everything in sight. He must be burning up calories just standing there, Jennifer thought, though he was rarely "just standing."

He didn't want to return to the pediatrician, but he conceded to her because she promised that if he did, she'd return his car keys, which she'd confiscated the morning after he'd disappeared for a whole day. She didn't intend to keep her promise, but she knew it was the only way.

Now, Alex's leg jiggled furiously as Dr. Morgan listened to his heartbeat, asking him to breathe long and deep. The room was silent, save for the crinkling of white paper under Alex's seat, and Jennifer was biting the inside of her cheek to keep herself from launching into every behavioral symptom that had brought them here.

Finally, Dr. Morgan asked, "And how have you been feeling since you were last here, Alex?"

She pulled a round stool from beneath the counter and sat down, adjusting its height as she did. She fixed Alex with a thoughtful, focused gaze.

"Good!" he said. "I mean, much better than before. It's weird—I think about how I felt, you know, how depressed I was, and it seems like another person. So I guess that means the meds are working, right?"

"Hmm," Dr. Morgan said. "Well, let's see. How have you been sleeping?"

Alex frowned. "I haven't been, I guess. It bothered me at first, because it was just weird, but now it feels cool, like I don't even need it! I can get so much more stuff done now."

"Stuff?" Jennifer interrupted. "What kind of stuff?"

Alex shrugged. "Just a few projects I'm working on, Mom. It's not a big deal."

"I see," Dr. Morgan said. "So, high energy, sleeplessness . . . Any other mood changes that you've both noticed? Do you feel more irritable or agitated than usual, Alex?"

Alex's leg kept up its frenetic bouncing. "I don't know. I don't think so."

"You don't think so?" Jennifer said, letting out an incredulous laugh. "Alex, you threw a textbook against the wall the other day!"

For a moment, he looked baffled, as though he had no idea what she was talking about. Then he smiled and shrugged. "Yeah. I guess."

"And he's been sent home from school twice," Jennifer continued to Dr. Morgan, unable to stop now that she'd started. "He skipped a whole day earlier this week. He's been drinking a lot—"

"Not as much as you would if you could," Alex shot back.

Jennifer raised a hand to her face, pressing two fingers between her eyebrows. A headache was brewing. To Dr. Morgan, she said, "I've been sober for eighteen months and six days."

Dr. Morgan nodded and smiled kindly. "Alex," she said, "it's clear to me that you're experiencing some side effects of this medication. They may not feel *bad* to you, but they're impacting your life in a negative way. I want you to discontinue using this medication and start the one I'll prescribe today. Can you do that?"

Alex was blinking rapidly. It unnerved Jennifer.

"Okay," he said simply.

"Great. Let's go ahead and get you checked out." Dr. Morgan smiled and stood, opening the exam room door. Alex bolted through as if he'd been held captive. But when Jennifer went to pass through, Dr. Morgan took her gently by the elbow. "One more thing, Jennifer," she said. "I didn't want to say this in front of Alex—I think it should be a talk the two of you have—but I believe he should see a licensed child psychologist. Just to make sure we're on the right track here."

> A *child psychologist* is an individual with a doctoral degree (Ph.D.) who is licensed by individual states to practice psychology. He or she can provide psychological testing and evaluations, treat emotional and behavioral problems and mental disorders, and provide a variety of psychotherapeutic techniques. They are not able to prescribe psychotropic medications.

Jennifer felt a flash of foreboding as she looked at Dr. Morgan's concerned face—a sudden intuition that this, whatever this was, was going to be neither easy nor simple. A new prescription was only the beginning.

"I—I wouldn't even know where to start," Jennifer said.

"I'll give you a few referrals," Dr. Morgan replied, patting Jennifer's shoulder, "and you can see which will work best for you—your insurance, all that." After a moment, she added, "You'll be doing the right thing."

CHAPTER 3

"Is there any way we can get in sooner?" Jennifer asked, tapping her nails along the edge of her desk. She'd come into work—she was a part-time bookkeeper at a salon—early that morning, hoping for some quiet time alone to call the psychologist she'd researched the night before.

"I'm so sorry, but Dr. Burton doesn't have any new patient openings for a month. If you take this appointment and something opens sooner, I can make a note that you'd like us to contact you." The receptionist's voice was kind; clearly she understood the frustrations of parents calling to see a child psychologist. Her message also sounded carefully rehearsed, as if she had to give this speech to a new family each day.

Jennifer sighed. "Okay. We'll take it. And I'll pray that someone else has to cancel." She gave a weak laugh, which the receptionist returned.

"Great. I'll email over our intake forms. Also, it would be helpful if you could make a copy of the front and back of your son's insurance card. This way everything will be ready to go when you come in for your first appointment." The receptionist's cheery tone didn't waver.

"Thank you. See you soon."

Alex had started his new antidepressant the day

after their visit with Dr. Morgan. The few days since had passed relatively calmly, with Alex's mood shifting to one more quiet and internal. Over the weekend he'd stayed in his room, with the door closed. When Jennifer had peeked in once, he'd been fast asleep on top of his covers. Today was Tuesday, and he had begged her to let him stay home. He told her he felt his body was trying to catch up on the sleep he'd missed the previous two weeks. He sounded heavy and desperate. She'd kissed his forehead and agreed, and Alex had immediately pulled a pillow over his face and closed his eyes. Carefully, on her way out the door, she'd confiscated Alex's car keys, as well as the spare. At least she'd know he would be safe.

Jennifer was relieved to work uninterrupted through her lunch break. She was nibbling on the sandwich she'd brought with her, trying to check each item from her to-do list, when her office phone rang.

"Jennifer Magana," she answered, expecting a client or one of her bosses on the other line.

"Mom. Where are my keys?" Alex demanded.

"They're in my bag. You're sick today, so I didn't think you'd miss them."

"But Mom. I need—I need to get out of here. There's nothing here for me, and I have to get out. I need to go to the library. You don't want me to fall behind at school, do you?" Alex's voice was frantic, a far cry from the tone he'd used this morning.

"Alex, get some rest. I'll be home in a few hours. If you still need to get to the library, I can drive you." Jennifer bit her lip. Alex didn't respond well to no.

"You don't understand! I've got it! And I need the evidence to support my theory!" Alex exclaimed.

"Your theory?" Jennifer asked warily. "What theory?"

"There's a chemical in the brain that's produced—it's called DMT for short. Well, scientists have found that when it's introduced to the human body outside of the brain, it's one of the most powerful hallucinogens—more powerful than LSD. Through some simple sketches, I've discovered a way to mass-produce a lighter version of the chemical, which would open the doors to all sorts of experiments. Sometimes, it's called the 'spirit particle,' and it's regarded as holy in tribes in South America."

Jennifer was flummoxed. Her son was so bright—there was no doubt about that—but right now he just sounded . . . well . . . crazy. She closed her eyes. "Alex, do your research on the Internet, and I'll be home in a little while. I have to go back to work now."

"It's because you're not my real mom!" Alex exploded. "My real parents were geniuses like me! You don't get it because you can't!"

"Alex, I am your real mother. Come on now." Jennifer lowered her voice so that her coworkers couldn't hear the conversation. She was hurt and mortified. Where was this coming from? Only once before had Alex said she wasn't his real mother, and he was much younger then. Jennifer had dismissed it—as she'd dismissed a lot, she was realizing—as the typical concoction of a child. Who didn't think they were adopted, at one point?

"You can't be! There's no way I came from you!" Alex shouted. "My real mother would appreciate what I've discovered. My real mother would be able to understand my true genius. When I find her and prove you're lying, you're going to regret everything!"

I could just hang up, Jennifer thought. I could just put

down this receiver, and there would be nothing but silence in my office. I could get back to work, go to happy hour with the girls—no drinks, obviously—bring home takeout for dinner, and just pretend my life is normal. The sweet relief of her tempting thought quickly gave way to anxiety and guilt.

"Alex, I can't leave work right now. Get on the Internet. I'll be home as soon as I can. I love you. I am your real mother. I'll see you soon." Jennifer hung up the phone, despite Alex's cries of protest. The abrupt quiet filled her mind, silencing even the guilt that still weighed on her chest.

By three-thirty, Jennifer had caught up on work and gotten a good head start on a new project she was launching the following week. Exhausted, she knew that she should go home early but dreaded what she'd find. She sent a note that she'd be working from home the rest of the day and slowly collected her things.

Her body buzzed with anxiety on her drive, building to a climax that released slightly when she pulled into her garage—Alex's car was still in the driveway, so he'd clearly not tried to hotwire it to get out. She shook her head at those thoughts. Her life had become so lonely, so isolating. Clearly something was different about Alex, but how much of it could be brain based and genetic, and how much of it was because of her and Sebastian? Was it nature or nurture? Or was it both? She grabbed her bag from the passenger's seat and walked into the house, unsure of what could lie before her.

"Alex?" she called out. Hearing nothing but her voice echoing across the tile of the kitchen, her stomach sank. "Alex?"

She went upstairs, finding his bedroom door open and his room empty. Frantically, she dialed his cell phone. Straight to voicemail. Damn it! she thought. I should have come straight home! I should have—

Her thoughts were interrupted by the opening of the front door.

"Alex?" she called.

"Yeah, Mom?" Alex was breathless, but his voice sounded fine. Normal, almost.

Bounding down the stairs, Jennifer saw her son drinking from a water bottle, bent over at the waist. His face was red and shiny with perspiration, and his running shoes were tracking wet footprints inside the house.

"Where were you? I was so worried!" Jennifer exclaimed.

"I just went for a run, Mom. It's good thinking time," Alex responded, taking another sip from his water bottle.

"I'm just glad you're home," Jennifer said, as Alex rushed past her and up the stairs. "Where are you going?"

"Time to get back to my computer. I think I've figured everything out!" he called, closing the door to his room with a definite, but preoccupied, slam.

By Sunday morning, Alex's renewed, ferocious energy hadn't abated. When Jennifer padded into the kitchen to make her coffee at six a.m., her habitual wake-up time even on the weekends, she was shocked to find the light on and Alex pacing circles around the table.

"You're up early," Jennifer said. When Alex looked at her, Jennifer could see the dark rings around his eyes. "Or late?" she ventured.

Alex shook his head. "I slept, Mom. I'm just motivated. I feel like I'm on the verge of something so great that I won't even have to do my senior year. This could be so

huge that they'll just waive me out of the school require-
ments. That fat-ass principal will just say 'Here you go,
son!' They're just going to give me a high school diploma
when I get this. I've been up thinking all night. Besides,
I'm fine. I'm full of energy. I'm not even tired." Alex continued pacing the table's circumference. Jennifer was
getting dizzy watching her son move in circles. "It's possible," he said, "that I don't even need sleep. Maybe none
of us do. Imagine what the world would be like if nobody
needed to sleep! I think I'll work on that next. But I need
to solve this first. One thing at a time, you know?"

"Well, all right, Alex." Jennifer tried to keep her tone
neutral, but her stomach was sick with worry.

He was such a bright kid. He'd started speaking in full
sentences at eighteen months old. As Jennifer started the
coffeepot, she thought about how Alex really could dis-
cover something that would make him famous—that he
really might be a genius. If only he could get his moods
under control. One moment he was distressed and sad
and the next he seemed on top of the world. He just
needed to even out.

Jennifer thought back to what Sebastian had told
her about his father. He remembered sitting on a blanket with his siblings in their big backyard, their father
and his friends jamming, playing Led Zeppelin songs
that were already seven minutes long for close to fifteen. Alejandro would catch Sebastian's eye and wink
sometimes, just as he dove into the intricacies of a completely improvised guitar solo. Sebastian's heart would
swell with pride. "Look at Papi!" he would say to his
mother, his hazel eyes reflecting the pride in hers. The
party would last until three a.m., when Sebastian would

briefly awaken as his father carried him to bed from the place on the floor where his little body was finally overcome with exhaustion. That's the thing, isn't it? Jennifer thought as she poured her first cup. Genius comes at a cost.

Jennifer took her cup back to bed, where she turned on the TV and promptly fell asleep again. She awoke to the sound of crashing in the kitchen, as though each pot in her cabinet had jumped from the shelf and banged to the floor. Heart pounding, she raced to the kitchen to find Alex digging through the lazy Susan, discarding pots and muttering about how they were inadequate.

"Alex! What's going on?" Jennifer asked, her eyes wide.

"These pots are all useless!" Alex cried. "I'm so close, but I don't have what I need to confirm my theories. These are all just fucking useless!" He picked up a stockpot and threw it against the refrigerator. The clanging echoed and left a small dent in the stainless steel door.

"Calm down! Please. Let's just take a day off from experimenting. Today, let's just order a pizza and find some documentaries on Netflix. You love watching those." Jennifer's voice was pleading. She would do anything to calm Alex down.

"You just don't get it, do you?" Alex turned to his mother, and she could see the cold rage in his eyes. "You're so jealous of my brilliance that you can't handle the possibility of my breakthrough. You've taken away my car keys. You're keeping me at home so that I can stay in your box. You should have thought about that when you stole me. When you stole me from my real parents! I don't have proof yet, but I think I found them online. They're theoretical physicists at MIT. I have to get out of this hellhole early so that I can go to MIT with evidence that I am theirs! I belong with them, not here!"

Jennifer backed away from her son. He was further gone than she'd ever seen before. "Alex, you need to take a few deep breaths. Everything is fine. I'm not trying to distract you from your work. I understand that it's very important." She edged backwards into the dining room until her calves met a chair. She squeezed herself between it and the wall.

Alex rushed her. "Don't placate me! You need to admit the truth! I don't belong to you! You're jealous of my potential! Say it! Say it, damn it!" By the time the words had come out of Alex's mouth, he had his forearm against Jennifer's neck, pinning her against the wall. Her eyes went wide as Alex pulled his left arm back, poised to make direct contact with her face. Everything happened so fast that when the boom resonated through the house, Jennifer wasn't sure how badly she was hurt. She felt a flake of drywall graze her cheek, and Alex released her from his grip. Opening her eyes (and when had she closed them?), she was stunned to see a fist-sized dent in the wall next to her head. Alex was off, rummaging through her purse on the kitchen counter, where he grabbed his car keys and ran out the front door.

Jennifer sank to her knees. She wasn't going to try to stop him. In shock, she didn't remember getting up or dialing Sebastian's cell number, only that half an hour later, her ex-husband was there, holding her on the couch as she cried.

"I can't do this," Jennifer said. "I can't be afraid of my own son. I can't feel unsafe in my home. I don't know what to do, but I know it isn't this. Can he—maybe he can stay with you for a while? Just this week. I just need some time—some time to . . ." Jennifer trailed off, hearing the babble of her own voice, aware that she wasn't making any sense.

"I'm sorry," Sebastian said quietly. "I didn't know it was this bad."

Jennifer sniffled and pulled away from the weight of Sebastian's arm around her shoulder. For a moment, she wanted to yell at him. But she was just too tired.

"He needs help," Sebastian said. "Okay? I admit it. I didn't want to link him with my father; I wanted him to have a better life. To have better opportunities. No labels. But obviously Alex is only getting worse." Sebastian's voice cracked, and he looked helplessly at Jennifer. "And I haven't helped at all."

The admission loosened something in Jennifer's chest, just slightly eased the anger she'd been harboring toward Sebastian for years now.

"I'll see if we can leave a message for the psychologist," Jennifer said. "The one we have an appointment with in three weeks. Maybe he can at least give us some guidance."

Jennifer knew that there was more to Sebastian's longtime denial of Alex's problems than the fear that he wasn't a good enough parent. She was starting to understand the complex and toxic blend of love and resentment one could find herself imprisoned in when someone so close to her heart suffered with mental illness. My son suffers with mental illness, she repeated to herself. It was the first time she'd admitted it to herself so directly, and it was devastating.

Shakily, Jennifer dialed the psychologist's office, which

patched through to his answering service. "If this is an emergency, please dial 911 immediately," the recording greeted her before asking her to hold for the after-hours answering service. Her heart broke at the number of times that she'd taken those words for granted.

Seven minutes after leaving an urgent message for Dr. Burton, Jennifer's phone rang with a blocked number on her caller ID.

"Hello?" she answered, almost breathless.

"Yes. This is Dr. Burton. I'm returning your call." The psychologist's voice was low and calm, and she grasped hold of it. Without preamble, Jennifer explained how her son was a new client and then described the events of Alex's week, each moment compounded by the need to explain all the backstory, expanding the call into ten minutes before she finally got into the day's events.

"Did he say or do anything that makes you concerned he may be a danger to himself or others?" Dr. Burton asked.

Jennifer thought about it. Alex could have hurt her—he'd thought about it, surely—but he didn't. And he'd never threatened to hurt himself. "No," she said finally, "but it's the closest it's ever been."

"Okay. If things change and you are worried about danger to self or others, then you need to call 911. Also, I can rearrange my schedule to see him first thing in the morning. Can you have him at my office at . . . eight-thirty?" Dr. Burton asked, as though he were looking through his calendar.

"Thank you, yes!" Jennifer cried. "Thank you so much, Dr. Burton. We'll be there."

Jennifer hung up the phone and looked over at Sebastian,

who had closed his eyes and was resting his head on the triangle of his hands.

"We're getting in tomorrow," Jennifer said softly. "Will you come with us?"

Sebastian raised his head and gave her a sad smile. "Yes."

· · ·

When the sun began to set, Jennifer's already nervous stomach twisted into deeper knots. Alex was still out, and they didn't know where he was. He'd left his cell phone at home, and she had no idea how to find him. She thought she'd give him space to calm down, but their fight had been almost seven hours earlier. Sebastian had gone home long ago.

Unsure what to do, she walked into the kitchen and set the kettle to make some chamomile tea. It was times like these when she most wished she weren't what she was—an alcoholic. She wished so desperately that she could be a person who could have just one vodka tonic. Just one. Cool and crisp and sharp, making the edges of her fear a little less sharp. Just one and then she'd stop. Why was it so easy for other people to stop and so impossible for her?

A key in the front door made Jennifer jump. Alex stumbled in, smiling widely. He reeked of cigarette smoke and some kind of strange, boozy–Hawaiian Punch.

"Hey, Mama!" Alex said. "I went to . . . uh, I went to Bettany's house. We worked on an English project." Alex giggled before his eyes got wide and he curled over to vomit.

"Damn it, Alex," Jennifer said, rushing over to her son. "Tell me you didn't drive."

Alex's body heaved once more before he wiped his chin and looked up at his mother. "I'm not drunk. I was working on a school project. Must have eaten some bad Chinese food."

Jennifer swallowed past an urge to heave at the obvious smell of regurgitated alcohol. She wrapped her arm around her son's waist. "You need to get to bed. Let me help you up the stairs."

That her son could look her in the eye and lie broke her heart. But she didn't have the energy to call him on it tonight. If there was a bright side to Alex's actions that afternoon, at least he would sleep tonight, finally. She would get him up in the morning and take him to Dr. Burton. He wouldn't have time to complain or plot a way out of it.

Carefully, Jennifer helped Alex up the stairs. She pulled off his vomit-splattered t-shirt, but Alex shrugged off her attempts to help him into a clean one. He was snoring in moments. Pushing his curls back off his forehead, Jennifer leaned in to give him a soft kiss just above his eyebrow. His sleeping face reminded her of the toddler who'd insisted on crawling into bed next to her. She'd awaken to his sweet breath in her face and just watch him, considering the little person snuggled next to her. She'd fretted all through her pregnancy, worried about her capacity and readiness to be a mother, but when he came into the world, pink and screaming, the pain of what felt like lost years of youth melted away, surrounded by the new hope this little life brought. Although the road to delivering Alex from his mind might be arduous, bringing him, perfect and shining, into the world would happen again. It had to.

CHAPTER 4

When Iris, the receptionist at Dr. Burton's office, unlocked the front door, the Magana family was waiting for her. Tension filled the air, making it hard to breathe. Almost in slow motion, Jennifer and Sebastian took their seats. Alex chose to sit across from them, tapping a beat on his blue-jeaned thigh.

"Mr. and Mrs. Magana?" Iris smiled at them. "I'll need to collect those intake forms from you. I'll also need to get a copy of your insurance card and a copy of your driver's license."

Jennifer watched her ex-husband tensely walk to the receptionist's desk. She was still such a wreck, feeling as though she could dissolve at any moment. But that was why they were here—to get help. Sebastian returned, stuffing his wallet into his back pocket. His hazel eyes were narrowed with focus, and she realized he was as invested as she was in getting Alex help. For the first time in a long time, she felt lucky. She knew plenty of other divorced women who wouldn't be able to say the same in this situation.

George Michael's "Careless Whisper" came over the small radio Iris had behind her desk, and when the saxophone solo started, Alex began pantomiming the action.

Iris looked up from her computer screen and saw Alex, holding an invisible sax. She gave a small smile, and with just that little encouragement, Alex stood and went all out, moving his body to the rhythm. Jennifer and Sebastian looked up, both taken by surprise. He hammed it up, putting down his saxophone and mouthing the chorus: "I'm never gonna dance again. Guilty feet have got no rhythm." Jennifer couldn't help herself; she laughed, and the laughter was cathartic. After the past twenty-four hours, she needed to be reminded of her charming and charismatic son. Damn it, he could be tough, but damn it, he could be funny. She smiled at Alex, happy to be reminded of the son she recognized.

Just then, Dr. Burton opened the door into the waiting room and surveyed the scene. "Good morning," he said, introducing himself with a smile. "Would you folks please follow me?"

Sebastian and Jennifer stood and shook the psychologist's hand, and Alex dropped his act and followed suit. A white-noise machine buzzed as the family was led down a hall and into an office with two armchairs and an overstuffed couch. Jennifer glanced at Alex to see that his eyes were hooded with apprehension. While he'd reluctantly agreed to see a psychologist when he thought it was a month out, Jennifer and Sebastian had near-ambushed him with this morning's visit. It wasn't ideal, but then, none of this was.

"Sit wherever you'd like." Dr. Burton motioned to the sofa and the chairs. Jennifer took a seat on the couch next to a squat black space heater. Alex sat beside her, and Sebastian and Dr. Burton took each of the chairs. The furniture created a circle, and Jennifer was startled to find that the proximity and eye contact made her anxious. Dr. Burton looked over the family, keeping his gaze neutral before he fixed his eyes on Alex. "It's very nice to meet all of you. I know we've had an appointment scheduled, and Mrs. Magana, we talked briefly on the phone, but tell me more—how can I help you?"

Jennifer and Sebastian looked at each other and then away. No doubt, Jennifer thought, they were each hoping the other—or even Alex—would start.

No one spoke.

"Alex, I understand you enjoy science," Dr. Burton said, smiling at him as he referenced the paperwork he held in his hands. Dr. Burton's eyes were almost obstructed by thick glasses and bushy gray eyebrows, but the electric blue stood out.

"I do. I love chemistry," Alex replied.

"That's wonderful! I tell you, I had to take some chemistry classes as an undergraduate, and they pummeled my GPA." Dr. Burton chuckled. "Is there an area of chemistry you're most interested in?"

Alex lit up, and Jennifer cringed, anticipating what was coming.

"You're a doctor. You're aware of dimethyltryptamine? DMT, for short?" Without waiting for Dr. Burton to respond, Alex launched into his theory about mass producing a lighter version of the chemical. Jennifer winced and looked at Sebastian, who stared at Alex as though he were a stranger. "I mean, this is the chemical that's active when we dream. When we dream! Can you imagine what could be done if it were actually used intentionally? The—the clarity people could find?"

"That's fascinating, Alex." Dr. Burton leaned closer,

elbows on his knees. "When did you think of this?"

Jennifer crossed her legs, impatient. While she was glad that Dr. Burton was hearing these wild ideas first-hand, she didn't know why he was probing into the details. Surely this wasn't relevant. They should be talking about the mood swings, the violent temper.

"Well, honestly, it started with a documentary that I saw on Netflix," Alex said. "Then I pulled out my chemistry textbook and started studying the structure of the molecule. I just want to help people, Dr. Burton. I just want to find a way to make people happy—to help them find meaning. Because all of this—this you're-a-kid-until-you're-eighteen-and-you-have-to-follow-a-certain-path crap is just *killing* the creativity in our society. It's just beating the genius out of all of us. You know?" Alex maintained intense, unblinking eye contact with Dr. Burton.

"I see," Dr. Burton said. "Let's switch gears for a moment. It sounds like things didn't go so well between you and your mom yesterday. Can you tell me about that?"

Jennifer could feel Dr. Burton's eyes on her as her skin flushed with anxiety. She'd known, of course, that they would need to have this conversation with the psychologist, but she wasn't looking forward to Alex's response. She said a silent prayer that he wouldn't explode.

"She . . . I know I was wrong." Alex looked over at Jennifer, who pressed her lips together and gave a small nod. "I remember feeling like she wasn't taking me seriously, but I—I don't know why I got so mad. It doesn't even feel real." Alex looked into his hands, his eyebrows furrowed. "But I know it was because, well—" He gestured at the room. "Here we are. Here I am, with a shrink."

"Alex, would you mind talking to me privately for a

little while?" Dr. Burton asked, casting a look at Sebastian and Jennifer.

Alex shrugged. "I guess."

Jennifer hesitated. She felt anxious and protective. But Sebastian stood, looking at her.

"Come on, Jen," he said. To the doctor, he added, "We'll be in the waiting room. Just let us know if you need us back in here."

When they were again seated outside, Jennifer looked at Sebastian. "What do you think?"

"I think he seems to know how to talk to Alex, which is something. God only knows what the kid's going to tell him, though," Sebastian said, wiping his palms on his dress slacks.

"I know. I'm worried about that too." The crease between Jennifer's eyes deepened as she considered what Alex might tell the psychologist. She envied the mothers who no longer worried about their children saying inappropriate or humiliating things in public.

Sebastian reached into his pocket and pulled out his smartphone. He began the steady click click click of his thumbs, and then the text message ding sounded. Jennifer picked up a *National Geographic* magazine from the table to distract herself from the familiar pang: Sebastian was probably texting his wife. Maybe asking for an update on their child. Maybe updating her on the problems with his other son. Jennifer wondered when this new life of his would stop being so painful to her.

. . .

The psychologist's office isn't what Alex expected. He thought he'd see a big leather couch and gleaming wooden bookshelves, with thick, old-school books—the ones with fabric covers and gold lettering that are always just for show. He imagined the psychologist would rub his beard a lot and pretend to take notes, when really he would be doodling, just drawing circles over and over again or drawing women's breasts or something creepy like that. But the couch Alex is sitting on is some kind of tweed, and the bookshelves are simple and basic but take up the whole wall, with some books stacked horizontally in front of the vertical ones, as if Dr. Burton pulled them out for reference but didn't bother sliding them back in neatly. This comforts Alex, for some reason. He appreciates that true intelligence isn't always orderly; it doesn't concern itself with appearances. Dr. Burton himself is dressed in a flannel shirt and pullover sweater with slacks. His eyebrows are mad-scientist crazy, but his gray hair is short. No beard.

"Alex," Dr. Burton says, "before we begin, I want you to know that anything you tell me in here is confidential. I will not repeat anything to your parents *unless* I feel there's a possibility of you hurting or killing yourself or someone else, or if you're having sex with someone over eighteen. Okay?"

Alex evaluates Dr. Burton for a moment. His mind snagged on the doctor's last comment: sex with someone over eighteen. It hasn't happened, but Alex feels a twitch of excitement at the thought. Finally, he nods.

"Alex, I've got the paperwork here that your mom filled out," Dr. Burton says, lifting the folder in his lap, "but I'd like to hear directly from you what you've been experiencing."

Alex juts out his chin. "What do you want to know?"

"Well, you started taking medication because you were feeling symptoms of depression, correct?" When Alex nods, Dr. Burton continues. "Can you tell me about those feelings? When did they first start?"

Alex tries to think back, but his mind is racing again—it wants to go *forward*, not backwards. What's the point of going backwards? No one ever made progress that way. And when he tries, everything is watery and indistinct. He remembers the depression, of course. But here, with that electricity buzzing beneath his skin, he can't quite make it real.

"I remember feeling worthless," Alex says, closing his eyes, trying to focus. "Like I was just wasting space, you know? I remember feeling like there was no future for me. I couldn't imagine myself *doing* anything. I didn't even want to get out of bed. My body hurt. I just wanted to be alone, in the dark. I cried a lot," he admitted softly. "It felt . . . endless. Like I was going to feel that way forever. Which just goes to show," he said, opening his eyes, "the mind can convince you of anything. Which is why I want—"

Dr. Burton smiles and gently interrupts. "Alex, how long did those periods of sadness last at one time?"

Alex frowns. "I don't know."

"A day? A week? Months?"

"Maybe a week," Alex says. "Then I'd snap out of it. But when I was *in* it, I never believed it would stop."

"That must have felt frightening, the possibility of being trapped in that state."

Alex nods, feeling strangely somber.

"And Alex, when you *did* 'snap out of it,' as you say, what happened then? What was your mood like then?"

Alex shrugs. "Back to normal, I guess. Well, normal for *me*," he amends. "I'm not like everyone else. Once I get out of that bullshit depression, I'm on top of the world. I have tons of energy and ideas and I don't even need to sleep. I mean, I don't even get *tired*! I can go for days without sleeping, and it doesn't affect me. It just lets me work on my projects without stopping, which is awesome because I don't have that recovery period that normal people have. Like you," he says, leaning forward. "I bet when you get here in the morning, you need a cup of coffee to get started, right? Maybe a few cups. And then you have to go over your notes and remind yourself where you were the day before and which crazy people you're seeing today. But me, I don't have to do any of that. My battery is always fully charged. I'm like the optimum-functioning human being. Hey—you should probably study me. I bet you'd learn a lot."

Dr. Burton is nodding, never taking his eyes off Alex though his pen is moving over the notepad he holds above the folder. "I see," he says. "And, Alex, when you're in this mood—when you're sort of revved up, as it sounds like—what do you *do*? You work on your projects . . . What else?"

Alex narrows his eyes. He feels suddenly as if Dr. Burton is trying to trick him, but he's not sure how. "I run . . ." he says. Give him something safe, something boring.

"For how long? How far?"

The specifics of Dr. Burton's questions are starting to annoy him. How should he know all these details? What does it matter? "I don't know, hours," he says. "Two or three hours, so if I run a seven-minute mile, which I do, what's that, seventeen miles in two hours, almost twenty-six in three."

As Alex says this, he's surprised. He thinks of the blisters on his feet, the way two of his toenails have blackened and become loose. He thinks of how goddamn *thirsty* he is afterwards. But in truth, he never realized he ran that much. He's proud of his endurance but uncomfortable with his lack of awareness.

"Well, that's very impressive, Alex," Dr. Burton says, and Alex relaxes a little. "Anything else? Do you ever drink or do drugs? Again, anything you say in here will be kept confidential."

"I drink," Alex says. "I like drinking. There's nothing wrong with that."

"Okay. How often do you drink? How much?"

Alex's annoyance flares again. "I don't know! It's not like I keep track."

"Every day, would you say? Three times a week?"

"Whenever I can," Alex says defiantly. "It's not like I have money all the time, and my mom doesn't keep alcohol in the house. You know she's an alcoholic," he adds.

Dr. Burton nods. "She did make note of her history in the paperwork. And what about drugs, Alex?"

"I don't *need* drugs," Alex says. He stretches his arms out wide. "People take drugs to feel the way I feel all the time."

Dr. Burton makes a note. "Do you ever feel like you're being impulsive?" he asks. "Do you ever decide to do something in the moment that's a bit out of character for you? Or maybe catch yourself doing something you didn't really intend to do?"

"Like what?" Alex asks warily. He feels, again, as though he's being tricked. As though Dr. Burton wants to catch him in something.

Dr. Burton shrugs and crosses his legs. "It could be anything, really."

For a few moments, the room is silent save for the low whir of the space heater, which makes the air smell almost burnt, but not in a bad way. Alex looks down at his hands to find that they're shaking. He's not sure when he last ate. A disjointed stream of images flashes in his mind, though he can't place them in time: driving, being surprised he's whole cities away from home; playing chicken on a two-lane road, staring right into the high beams of an oncoming truck and sweating, adrenaline rushing, then laughing and laughing when the truck finally swerves onto the shoulder with an enraged bleating of the horn; going out to the frozen lake (when was this?) and walking across its surface in the dark, knowing that there were thin spots in the ice and waiting for the fall, expecting it, somehow knowing that he wouldn't drown and wouldn't suffer hypothermia because he never feels cold anymore—he's impervious, and he wants to prove it; cruising slowly through the part of town his mom calls bad but he thinks is just honest, smiling at the hollowed-out women in fake fur coats, wishing desperately he had just a few bucks to invite one of them into his car.

"Alex?" Dr. Burton says gently.

The images are confusing. Alex has the sense that he's accessing someone else's memory, rather than his own. "Yeah," he says. "I do that sometimes. The impulsive thing. I—" He swallows, feeling slightly nauseated. "Dr. Burton, is something wrong with me? Because all of that, it just feels normal. It just feels like who I am. But thinking about it makes me feel . . . weird."

"Weird, how?"

"Like . . . like I'm not quite sure I'm actually *choosing* any of it. You know?" The moment Alex says those words, tears spring unexpectedly to his eyes. Dr. Burton glances down at his paper while Alex sniffs and wipes them away. Alex appreciates that.

"Alex, thank you for being honest with me today. I just have one more question for you for now: Since you started taking antidepressants, has this mood, these symptoms—the sleeplessness, high energy, impulsivity, irritability—lasted longer than usual?"

Alex doesn't even remember when he started the medication. It feels like ages since he felt low. He nods. "It's been a few weeks, pretty constant. Except for maybe a few days after I started this new med. But then I went back to normal."

Dr. Burton nods. "Okay. If it's all right with you, I'd like to call your parents back in."

···

After half an hour, Alex emerged into the waiting room. "He wants to talk to you now," he said. "Guess it's my turn to wait."

"Okay. You going to be okay out here?" Jennifer asked, though Alex had already pulled out his phone and stuffed his headphones into his ears. Jennifer met Sebastian's eyes as they walked the hallway back to the psychologist's office. They didn't speak, but Jennifer felt some comfort that they were there together.

After they'd taken their seats, Dr. Burton smiled at them. "Thank you for letting me share some time with your son. He's a bright young man. Very articulate."

"Thank you," Jennifer replied cautiously.

"I noticed in Alex's paperwork that his grandfather," Dr. Burton looked over the form in front of him, "your father, Sebastian, had suspected bipolar disorder."

Sebastian's body tensed. In a thin voice, he replied, "My psychologist and I suspect that he did. I went through some therapy after my mother died, and that's the theory we worked with. My father is also gone, so he can't answer for himself."

"I'm sorry." Dr. Burton's voice was sincere.

"Is that what you think is wrong with Alex?" Jennifer asked, horrified.

"Well," Dr. Burton said, "Alex clearly has issues with his moods, and what he described to me makes me worry that he has more than just depression. Bipolar disorder has periods of depression but also hypomanic or manic symptoms. It can be easily misdiagnosed as depression. In fact," he added, "it takes up to seven years for most people with bipolar disorder to reach a correct diagnosis because the symptoms cross over with depression and ADHD, even oppositional defiant disorder."

> **Bipolar disorder** causes unusual shifts in mood, energy, activity levels, and the ability to carry out day-to-day tasks. These mood shifts are different from the normal ups and downs that everyone goes through from time to time.

> **Mania** is a term used to describe a series of symptoms that occurs in individuals with bipolar disorder I. Symptoms can include feeling high or having an overly happy mood, or significant irritability along with decreased need for sleep; being easily distractible; feeling as if one's thoughts are racing; talking faster or feeling pressure to keep talking; impulsivity; psychotic symptoms (hallucinations, delusions, or paranoia); having an unrealistic belief in one's abilities; and increased activity or restlessness.

"Oh, my God," Jennifer said. She looked at Sebastian, feeling as if she could actually vomit. "Ever since he was a kid, his teachers recommended that we get him checked out for those things . . ." She trailed off. "But we never did."

"You never told me that," Sebastian said, his voice even but steely.

"You know why," Jennifer retorted.

"Sebastian, I asked about your father because bipolar disorder does have a hereditary component," Dr. Burton said. "If Alex's grandfather suffered from it, it's more likely that Alex is suffering from it as well. We need to continue to look at this."

"What does that mean?" Sebastian asked.

Jennifer looked at her ex-husband. She recognized that gruff tone. He was in pain. He felt guilty. In the happier days of their marriage, she would have reached over to put a gentle hand on his forearm, just to let him know she was there. Today, she just sat quietly.

"I'd recommend you seeing a licensed child and adolescent psychiatrist. If this is bipolar disorder, medication is an important and helpful part of the treatment plan."

> A **child and adolescent psychiatrist** is an individual with a medical degree (M.D.), licensed by individual states to practice psychiatry. He or she can provide evaluations, as well as treat emotional and behavioral problems and mental disorders by prescribing psychotropic medications and by providing other psychotherapeutic techniques.

"Medication," Jennifer said, feeling as if she were coming up from underwater. "But that's what brought us here. At least, partially. I'm convinced that Alex's mood the last few weeks is because of the antidepressants."

Dr. Burton nodded. "And you're probably right. Antidepressants can exacerbate the manic symptoms in bipolar disorder. Your pediatrician meant well, but I'd say she was a bit out of her element. A psychiatrist will be able to evaluate Alex and suggest a course of psychotropic medication that has been proven to help with bipolar disorder."

> **Psychotropic medications** are any medications used to treat mental disorders. There are many types of psychotropic medications, including antidepressants, anxiolytics, mood stabilizers, stimulants, and antipsychotics. Psychotropic medication is often helpful for symptom reduction in bipolar disorder.

Jennifer exhaled long and slow, then drew in another breath. Her throat was in danger of closing, and she didn't want to cry. "Doctor," she said, trying to keep her voice steady, "if Alex does have bipolar disorder, is there . . . I mean, is there a *cure?*"

Dr. Burton sighed. "I know how hard this must be to hear," he said, "and how afraid you must be for your son. I wish I could say there is a cure, but there simply isn't. However, with medication, symptoms can be effectively managed. There are the horror stories, of course—the sad tales, such as that of your father"—he turned to Sebastian—"but there are also plenty of people with bipolar disorder who are able to successfully manage their symptoms. What I'm telling you is this: there is hope."

Sebastian was working his jaw, blinking hard. This time, Jennifer reached for him, and he let her hold his hand.

"Should we—" Sebastian cleared his throat. "Should we get Alex back in here?"

Dr. Burton nodded. "I'm going to give you all a referral for a psychiatrist. Dr. Coker, a colleague of mine, has treated several of my other patients. If you sign a release, I'll be able to discuss your son's case with him prior to your appointment to give him my thoughts. He would then meet with you and Alex, do his own assessment, and give you his thoughts on next steps. And I'd like to see you back in two weeks. Individual and family psychotherapy can be very helpful. When we meet next time, we'll talk more and work toward goal setting and an overall treatment plan."

> *Outpatient psychotherapy,* or "talk therapy," occurs in a clinic and is a way to treat people living with mental disorders by helping them understand their illness. It teaches people strategies and gives them tools to deal with stress and unhealthy thoughts and behaviors. Psychotherapy helps patients manage their symptoms better and function at their best in everyday life.

"Okay. Thank you," Jennifer said. She took a breath to compose herself, released Sebastian's hand, and rose to summon Alex.

CHAPTER 5

Bipolar disorder. Manic depressive. Extreme mood changes. Fragments of Dr. Burton's words echo in Alex's mind. His bedroom is dark, the shades drawn against the bright gray day. His mom collected the rest of the antidepressants Dr. Morgan prescribed, and now his body feels leaden, his brain soggy and full of grief. How can he have bipolar disorder? How can his mom actually believe that? Bipolar disorder—that's straight crazy. Those people should be locked up; they *are* locked up sometimes, aren't they? Or they're roving the streets, utterly unaware of how disconnected they are from reality. How can Alex possibly be among their ranks?

He stole a twenty from his mom's purse earlier and bought another bottle of Old Crow, plus some cigarettes. Usually when he smokes up here, he does it with his head half out the window, blowing the sharp fumes up toward the sky. But today he doesn't care. What's his mom going to say? Is she really going to add to the profound shittiness that is his life by removing one of the only things that brings him pleasure? He lights up a cigarette and inhales, holding the smoke in his lungs until they burn. This is what he loves about cigarettes and booze: they make him feel things. His heart rate picks up, just a little, just a pathetic echo of the electric buzz he used to feel. He can't imagine, now, summoning the energy to walk around the block, let alone run a marathon the way he was supposedly doing these past weeks. Now he doubts that that even happened, even though his feet tell a traumatic tale.

Alex's room is cold—it's always colder upstairs than down, even though heat is supposed to rise. He pulls the covers tighter around him and lifts the bottle to his lips. He appreciates its heft in his hands, the coolness of the glass, the glow of amber liquid that Alex doesn't see so much as imagines. The whiskey starts to warm him. Another long drag on his cigarette and swig of Crow and he's starting to feel better.

Bipolar disorder. What the ever-living fuck? What's he supposed to do with this? The life ahead of him stretches bleak as an empty bottle. He doesn't want to finish school. What's the point? It's not like he's going to college. Not like he's going to have a career, a family. That's for other people, people whose brains are whole and glistening with promise. His brain must be withered, the synapses or neurotransmitters or whatever fizzing out like a string of tired Christmas lights. How's he supposed to have a normal life, do what normal people do, if his *brain* is broken?

Alex feels the tears swell in his chest moments before the weeping begins. He puts out his cigarette on the plate on which his mother brought him a sandwich earlier, and tries to stop the choke of sobs by taking another shot of whiskey. The bottle clashes with his teeth, sending a sharp pain shooting to the back of his head. He lifts a finger to his mouth—fucking great. He chipped his left front tooth. He can't even drink right. The thought is unbearable.

Setting the bottle down on his bedside table, he pulls aside the shade to his window and lifts it. A swift chill pierces his t-shirt, raising gooseflesh. Outside, an awning slopes below his window. The ground is covered in snow, bearing slushy footprints. His, probably. The neighborhood of modest brown-brick homes looks flat and boring, like aisles of cages in a pet store. He wants to leap from the awning onto the snow below. Not to die or anything—the fall is too short for that, the snow too soft—but just to feel something. To remember what that's like. His visit with Dr. Burton was less than a week ago, but already, the memories of that energized time are faded and strange. Is that another thing wrong with him? He can't seem to maintain focus in his memories. Things happen, and then they nearly disappear.

Shivering, Alex closes the window and slides against the wall. He grabs the Old Crow again. It's already a third down. All he wants to do is sit here and finish it. He'll feel better when he does. He has to believe that.

• • •

Jennifer was amazed that Dr. Coker's office got Alex in that Friday. Sebastian couldn't take any more time off work that week, so Jennifer loaded Alex into her Suburban and took him to the doctor's office by herself. The radio buzzed with Alex's favorite mix of "old music," songs that had come out before he was born but that Jennifer and Sebastian had danced to in their early marriage. As Sublime's "Santeria" came through the speakers, Jennifer looked over at her son. His skin was slick and gray, his hair lank. He smelled like dirty laundry and booze. She'd know that day-after smell anywhere.

"I'm proud of you for coming today," she said quietly.

Alex looked at her, his eyes mournful. Then his gaze returned to the window, watching the trees flash by. Jennifer physically ached for him. Maybe it was wrong, but she preferred the manic Alex, the boy full of wild ideas and confidence, to this Alex, for whom she actually feared. That was the difference, she realized suddenly. When Alex was manic, she was afraid *of* him. When he was depressed, she was afraid *for* him. Both were torture.

Dr. Coker's office wasn't as homey as Dr. Burton's. Jennifer was reminded of the pediatrician's office. There were toys in the waiting room, and MIDI versions of children's lullabies played softly on overhead speakers. A blond receptionist who smelled like cigarette smoke and spearmint gum greeted Jennifer and Alex with a smile.

After signing in, they took a seat in the waiting room. The mesh of the black padded chairs scratched against Jennifer's bare arms. Alex's arms were crossed across his chest, telling Jennifer that he was not in a mood to chat, so she grabbed an outdated magazine to pass the time.

A youngish-looking middle-aged man opened the door to the reception area. His red hair and beard reminded Jennifer of a Viking. He introduced himself as Dr. Coker and called them back to his office.

"I've spoken with Dr. Burton and gotten records from Alex's primary care physician," Dr. Coker started, without preamble. "What I'd like to do now is talk to the two of you some more about your concerns. Then I'd like to speak to Alex alone and then call you back in, Mom."

Jennifer prickled. She'd always hated it when people treating her son called her "Mom," as if they couldn't bother to learn her name. But she allowed that she was anxious, and that probably made her irritable. She just nodded. Alex, sitting beside her on the small, tastefully neutral couch, said nothing.

Jennifer answered most of Dr. Coker's questions for the ten minutes that followed. They were all similar to what Dr. Burton had asked, save for a more intense focus on Alex's responses to the antidepressants. Alex was slumped against the sofa cushions as they talked about him, unresponsive.

"Okay, Mom," Dr. Coker said. "Thanks for helping to fill me in. If you don't mind, I'll take some time with Alex now."

"Sure," Jennifer said. She took Alex's hand and squeezed it. "Let me know when you want me back in."

In the waiting room, she pulled out her smartphone and texted Sebastian to distract herself: *Alex is a complete zombie today. It's heartbreaking.* She waited for a response, but nothing came.

Twenty minutes later, Dr. Coker poked his head through the door again. "Mrs. Magana?" He motioned for her to join him, and she wondered why he had suddenly switched to such a formal address.

Back in his office, Dr. Coker sat upright behind his desk, revisiting a folder.

"Alex and I had quite an interesting conversation," Dr. Coker said.

Jennifer swallowed nervously but was relieved when Alex spoke. "I wouldn't say interesting," he said. "But it was fine."

Jennifer raised an eyebrow at her son.

Alex shrugged, picking at a hangnail. "He asked if I ever thought about killing myself."

"Do you?" Jennifer asked, holding her breath.

Alex shook his head. "He also asked about Dad's dad." Alex started listing off the questions.

"We can talk about it later, Alex." Jennifer smiled and then directed her full attention to Dr. Coker.

"Dr. Burton mentioned that he thought your son is struggling with bipolar disorder, and I also believe that is accurate." Dr. Coker paused, as if waiting for a reaction. She only nodded. "There are two types of bipolar disorder: bipolar I and bipolar II. Are you familiar with the differences?"

Jennifer shook her head. "No."

"Bipolar disorder is a spectrum disorder. With bipolar I, which is the most severe and disabling, you have episodes of mania. When you're manic," Dr. Coker said to Alex, "you'll have less need for sleep, which is a classic symptom. You'll be in an irritable mood or too happy of a mood, you'll talk faster, experience racing thoughts, go from one project to the next without finishing things. You'll feel like an Energizer Bunny."

Jennifer glanced at Alex, who seemed to be listening with interest.

"You'll have increased impulsivity," Dr. Coker continued, "and do things that are out of character—driving faster than usual, using alcohol or drugs, spending more money than usual. Some of my patients have even gone skydiving, despite being afraid of heights, when they're manic."

Alex registered the list of symptoms with an almost

imperceptible nod. He was recognizing himself in them, Jennifer thought.

"Now,"—Dr. Coker took on a more cautious tone—"some people with bipolar I also experience psychotic symptoms. That means they're unsure of what's real and what's not real. They may hear voices and see things other people don't hear or see. They can be paranoid, thinking someone is out to get them. They may think their phone is sending them special messages. They may think people can pull thoughts out of their head or put thoughts into their head. They have delusions of grandeur. That's mania. Typically, those symptoms last two or three days."

At this, Alex's face reddened. "I am not a fucking psychopath!" he said. He looked at Jennifer. "Mom! Do you hear this? Do you seriously think this is me?"

Before Jennifer could answer, Dr. Coker said calmly, "Alex, no one is calling you a psychopath. That is a completely different diagnosis. And as I said, only *some* patients with bipolar I experience such symptoms."

Jennifer remembered Alex calling her at work, yelling that she wasn't his real mother. She couldn't meet her son's eyes. "Dr. Coker, please go on."

Dr. Coker shifted in his seat, crossing his legs at the ankle. "As you know, mania is only one part of the cycle. The next part is depression—periods of up to two weeks experiencing feelings of worthlessness and hopelessness, losing interest in activities that are usually pleasurable, a deep sadness you can't shake. It's this that led you to originally seek help, which is quite common. Especially in bipolar II, which is a less severe version of what I've described, a first diagnosis of depression is fairly typical."

Alex crossed his arms, sulky and withdrawn after his

outburst. Jennifer reached over to touch his shoulder, but he pulled away. She sighed.

"What would you recommend, Dr. Coker?"

"I'd like for Alex to continue to see Dr. Burton. In order to achieve symptom reduction and enhance the effects of therapy, I'd also like to prescribe some medication for Alex—a mood stabilizer to start out. This particular mood stabilizer," he said, addressing Alex, "is something that will work by balancing the neurotransmitters in your brain. It will help to keep you from cycling between mania and depression, or times of feeling really high or really low. It can improve your mood, your alertness, and the way you interact with other people. I'll also prescribe a sleep medication, just in case you have any problems settling down at night. Use it as needed, but see how you do without it first."

> *Mood stabilizers* are a type of psychotropic medication used to treat bipolar disorder. This medication may also be used to treat other mental disorders as deemed appropriate by a physician, including depressive disorders and psychotic disorders.

Jennifer frowned. "Sleeplessness was a side effect of the antidepressants, and he didn't sleep for days at a time."

"More," Alex muttered.

"More," Jennifer repeated. "So what makes you think this is a better option?"

"Well, while antidepressants can be incredibly helpful to those with unipolar depression—that is, only depression—they can cause shifts into manic or hypomanic episodes in those, especially adolescents, with bipolar disorder. A mood stabilizer, on the other hand, is the first-line treatment specifically for those with bipolar disorder."

Jennifer nodded, satisfied. "So it sounds like difficulty sleeping is a potential side effect. Are there others we should know about?"

All medications, including over-the-counter medications, have the potential for side effects. Working closely with a physician can minimize the chance of having significant side effects. Remember, most medication side effects are mild and occur only during the first few days of starting a new medication or increasing the dose.

"I was coming to that. As with any medication," Dr. Coker said, "there can be unintended consequences, yes. The most common side effects are nausea or GI upset. Also, Alex, this is rare but very important." Dr. Coker looked Alex directly in the eye. "While this medication can reduce the risk of suicide sixfold, it can actually *cause* suicidal thoughts or actions in a very small number of patients. If, after taking the medication, you are having thoughts about harming yourself—if the idea even once crosses your mind—you need to communicate that to your parents immediately so they can contact Dr. Burton or me."

Jennifer's eyes widened. She felt sick. How could the line between treating an illness and potentially creating a whole new illness be so thin? She'd felt confident about their course of action up until this point, but now she felt a flash of fear: Was there a chance she was doing more harm than good by encouraging Alex to go on meds? Just look at how the antidepressants had worked out! But one glance over at Alex, who seemed to have barely registered Dr. Coker's words, filled her with resolve. If the alternative was to do nothing, to let him go on like this—well, it was no alternative at all. They didn't have any choice but to try.

"It's going to be very important that we keep in touch," Dr. Coker said. "I would like to see you and Alex in two weeks. Other patients find it helpful to keep a log of any changes they notice. That would be valuable to review at our next session. If you have any concerns before then—if you wonder, at any point, whether you should call me—then please, call me." Dr. Coker smiled reassuringly at Jennifer before shifting his focus to Alex again. "And it's going to be very important that you tell Mom how you're feeling. We need to know about any changes in mood and behavior, better or worse, that you experience."

"How long before I should start feeling a difference?" Alex asked. He looked up at Dr. Coker, and Jennifer read the exhaustion on his face.

"One to two weeks," Dr. Coker said. "Remember, though, that there is no magic pill. We're looking for immediate symptom reduction in order to allow therapy with Dr. Burton to be more effective and to allow you to return to your usual lifestyle."

"Am I going to have to take medication forever?" Alex asked.

Dr. Coker pursed his lips into an almost-smile. "Let's just take things one day at a time for now."

"Okay," Alex mumbled.

"Before you start the medication, I'm going to ask you to get some blood work done. Mom, I'll give you the paperwork. Also, if you haven't had a general physical exam in the last six months, you'll need one of those as well."

"Why?" Jennifer and Alex asked simultaneously.

"Though I'm confident that Alex meets the criteria for a diagnosis of bipolar I disorder, we need to do our due diligence and eliminate *any* other possible causes of these symptoms: vitamin D deficiency, thyroid problems, infection, that sort of thing."

"Could I have a brain tumor?" Alex burst out. "I mean, that could be a possibility, couldn't it?" For some reason, the thought seemed to galvanize him. He sat up straighter, looking beseechingly at Dr. Coker.

"It's an incredibly small possibility," Dr. Coker replied. "Highly, and I mean *highly*, unlikely."

Alex slumped back again. As if reading the question on Jennifer's face, he said, "At least if it was a brain tumor, we could either get it removed or I'd die soon."

"Alex!" Jennifer said. She shot Dr. Coker an apologetic glance, though she wasn't sure why she should be apologizing. "Don't say that."

Alex only shrugged.

CHAPTER 6

Alex did not have a brain tumor. His physical exam and blood work came back with the delightful results that he was, in fact, just crazy. At least, that was what he thought at the time, with the depressive's typical self-deprecating humor that poorly masked despair. He was able to start taking the new meds the week after seeing Dr. Coker, and he and his parents had their follow-up session with Dr. Burton that same week.

It took another week for Alex's depression to lift. He supposed maybe it was lifting a little each day, so gradually as to seem unnoticeable, until, one Saturday morning, he felt like going on a run. One of his toenails had fallen off and not completely grown back, but the blisters had healed over and his worn tennis shoes beckoned him from beneath his desk, where they had been hidden in shadow for what seemed like months.

"Mom!" he said, jogging downstairs.

"Alex! Are you okay?" His mother emerged from the kitchen, holding a cup of coffee. Her face, free of makeup, looked both old and young. Her eyes were wide with concern.

He smiled. "I'm fine. I'm going on a run. Just a short one."

His mother approached him, looked him up and down. "You're feeling . . . better?"

"Yeah," Alex said, shrugging. "I think so."

It was the first day in a long time—longer than Alex could recall—that he felt, well, *normal*. Or what he guessed normal people's normal felt like, anyway. He had energy, but he wasn't bouncing off the walls. As he jogged around the neighborhood, pulling his hood up around his face, he thought with some sadness that he was going to miss that feeling, that hyperstimulated sense of ecstasy and well-being. He wondered whether normal people ever got to feel that way. But if the trade-off was losing the depression, those days and nights of aching hell, it was worth it.

As weeks passed and the fog cleared, Alex felt he was emerging from a long, drug-induced sleep. Though his memories were still disturbingly indistinct, he knew he had done some weird shit when he was manic. And he recognized that the hopelessness he felt when he was depressed was deeply out of proportion with his life. It was scary, how good his brain could be at convincing him of things that weren't real.

One Sunday, when he and his mom were watching a documentary on Netflix, he said, "Hey, have I ever told you about this chemical called dimethyltryptamine? DMT?"

His mother turned to him, stricken. When he laughed, she swatted him on the shoulder, hard.

"Too soon?" he asked.

"*Never* would be too soon," she said. "Seriously, Alex, that was one of the scariest times of my life, hearing you talk like that. How much do you remember about it?"

He shrugged. "Not much. It's kind of like remembering you love pepperoni pizza, but you can't actually recall the taste."

They were quiet. Then, "Mom," he said, and she looked at him questioningly. "I'm sorry. For everything I put you through."

She smiled and sighed and tears rose to her eyes. She leaned in to hug him, and he hugged her back. "I'm just glad you're better," she said.

...

The thing about the meds is the side effects. Alex pees like a racehorse, all damn day, no matter how little water he drinks. He's been putting on weight, despite his regular runs. It's not *bad* or anything, but his face is fuller in the mirror and his jeans are fitting tighter. Then there's the hair loss. He thought he was imagining it at first, but nope—his thick head of wavy dark hair, which he shares with his father and shared with his grandfather before him, is changing. He notices it most in the shower, long strings catching in the slightly rusted drain, but he also wakes to find hair on his pillow and in his sheets, and paranoia has made him tug at it all day, each time coming away with five or six strands. At this rate, he'll be bald and fat by the time he turns eighteen.

He doesn't *decide* not to take his meds so much as, one day running late for school, he forgets. He remembers late in third period, and panic seizes him, as though he's about to turn into the Hulk. He considers asking to go to the nurse or calling his mom to bring the meds, but he tells himself it's only a few hours; it can't possibly be that big a deal.

And it's not. The day passes just as the day before did, in a slow-moving blur of biology, chemistry, English, and world history, a bad bean burrito at lunch, and frequent rushing to pee between classes. It's March, and though it's still cold outside, the sky is perfect and cloudless out the window, and he thinks he'll go for a run before attacking SAT prep.

The day passes so normally, so without incident, that the next day he forgets again. On the third day, he thinks mildly, Maybe I don't actually need them anymore . . . He decides to go a week without and see what happens. He imagines going back to Drs. Burton and Coker and saying, "It worked! I'm cured!" On the sixth day, he looks in the mirror and decides to buzz cut his hair. There are no clippers in the house, so he starts with kitchen scissors and takes it as short as the dull blades will let him. He finishes with a razor, bored but determined now that he's come this far. His mom, of course, freaks out when she sees him, but he says he's just getting ready for summer. He wants to try something different. She gives him an uncertain smile and tells him he looks handsome—older, like a soldier. She's lying, he can tell, but he doesn't care.

In his second week off the meds, he feels restless. He messages Bettany online after school, sees if she wants to get together. She says she's down for whatever, so he picks her up and they go to Mel's Liquors. She waits in the car because, she says, she has an honest face and no way she won't get carded. He looks at her, with her smudged black eyeliner and wine-colored lips, and laughs because it's not that she looks honest; she just has freckles.

They drive out to the lake, where they open the Old

Crow and share a joint Bettany brought before they move to the backseat. Alex can't get enough: the taste of booze on her tongue; the skunky smell of pot thick in the car; the warmth of her skin under his fingers; the realness of her legs around his hips, pulling him closer. Her dyed black hair falling in his face smells, unexpectedly, of something musty and papery, like a bookstore. They're not using a condom this time, which Bettany said is cool because she's on the pill, and Alex is lost in otherworldly pleasure. He doesn't want to stop, feels like he could do this for hours—for days, even. When Bettany eases herself off him, saying she's getting sore, he's wickedly disappointed. And when she looks down at him with raised eyebrows, asking what happened, wasn't she good enough today, he feels something like fury because he knows she's making fun of him. "Fuck you," he says, and she looks startled, then demands he take her home.

Bettany's neighborhood isn't far from his dad's condo, and as he drives off, leaving her in the front yard digging for her keys, he gets the idea to go visit him. He's never done that before, never just "stopped by," but Jesus—why not? They used to live together. Sebastian is his *dad*, and Alex has the right to see him whenever he wants. Even as Alex drives over, taking swigs of Old Crow as he goes, he's not sure why he's doing it. He doesn't have a burning desire to see his dad, really. He's not yearning for some father-son time. He just wants to show that bitch Sherry that he *can*. That essentially, their home is his home, too. That he's a part of their life, whether she likes it or not. It's about time she learn that.

Alex can't remember the gate code, so he calls his dad to ask. Sebastian sounds surprised and a little cautious, but pleased. "I'm about fifteen minutes away," he says, "but I'm sure Sherry's got something on the stove. Stay for dinner. I'll see you soon."

The gate slides creakily to the left after Alex punches in the code, and he wonders whether his dad hung up with him and called Sherry. He must have, because before he's even parked, the door to their condo opens and there she is, their son standing slightly behind her, holding both her legs.

She's hot, Alex has to admit. Long, strawberry blond waves and dark-rimmed glasses (he bets they aren't even prescription). She's wearing yoga pants and a long sweater, but he can tell she's still thin; no baby weight on her. He wonders whether his dad puts pressure on her to stay skinny. What's the use of having an affair, leaving your family, and getting remarried if your new young wife just gets fat? Alex imagines his dad can feel good about his choices as long as Sherry stays hotter than his mom. Which is pretty much a given since she's like twenty years younger.

"Alex!" Sherry calls as he gets out of the car. She's smiling. "It's so good to see you! Come in, it's chilly out. Don't you hate that? Still winter in spring?"

Alex shrugs. "It's not so bad," he says, following her inside.

"Caleb, look who it is," Sherry cooes at the kid. "Do you remember Alex?"

Caleb—Alex had seriously forgotten his name—stares up at him. When Alex moves a little closer, Caleb swings around to his mom's other leg, gripping it like a tree trunk in both arms and hiding his face.

"He's shy," Sherry says unnecessarily.

Alex looks around. Their place is bright and modern, all open spaces and whiteness: white cabinets in the kitchen, white chairs around a glass breakfast table, white shaggy throw rug under a glass coffee table, white couch with shocking purple throw pillows. Alex shakes his head. None of this looks like his dad. And how the hell do you have so much white when you've got a two-year-old?

"I've got some lasagna in the oven," Sherry says, moving into the kitchen. "It's a nice, easy thing to make that seems like you put a lot of effort into it." She laughs, and Alex knows then that she's nervous.

"Did my dad tell you I have bipolar disorder?" he blurts.

Sherry's back is to him as she reaches into the cabinet for a glass. She waits a second too long before turning around, a smile fixed on her face. "He says you've been doing a lot better," she says. "That's good, Alex. Only . . ."

"What?" he says. He takes the glass she offers him, but instead of waiting for her to pour him some water from the pitcher on the island, he pulls one of those mini-bottles of Scotch from his inside jacket pocket and sets the glass down.

Sherry winces. "Well, that. Do you really think you should be drinking on your medication? Drinking at all, for that matter? You're only seventeen."

"And you're only, what, five years older than me?"

Sherry stands up a little straighter. "Eight," she says, as if it matters. She glances at the clock on the oven. "Well, your dad should be here soon," she says. "I'm just going to give Caleb a bath. Make yourself at home."

Alex's head is spinning by the time he finishes the first mini-bottle and opens the second. He's not sure how much he and Bettany drank, but between the whiskey, pot, and cigarettes, he's feeling heavy but floaty, on high alert but relaxed, ready to laugh but also ready to fight. He makes his way through the kitchen, opening and closing cabinets. All of their dishes are white. What is this chick's deal? There's a tray on the counter with some mail, a key ring, a pair of earbuds, and some loose change—including, he sees with a grin, a twenty. He grabs the money, twenty-three dollars total, and sticks it in his pocket.

He continues his swaying search in the living room, feeling the pleasure of doing something strange, something out of the ordinary. He's not ordinary! Why did he ever want to be? Ordinary people don't make the world. They certainly don't control it. Ordinary people live in places like this, where everything is too white to touch. It's such bullshit.

In the TV armoire, Alex stumbles across a photo album. The photo in the front window is of him, when he was about six years old, grinning widely from a Popsicle-stained mouth. He doesn't remember that day, in particular, but he remembers summers. He remembers happiness. Taken aback, he flips through the photo album, and he finds pictures of the three of them together. He's surprised that his dad hasn't removed the ones with his mom in them, but it fills him with a surge of conviction that his dad still loves them—both of them.

Gripping the photo album, Alex runs through the condo, following the sound of running water. He finds Sherry and Caleb in a hall bathroom, laughing together. Nonslip stickers of ducks and birds make the water look pink.

"*We're* his real family!" Alex declares.

Sherry jumps, startled, and turns around. Her face

flushes with color, then quickly drains of it. "I'm sorry, what?" she asks.

Alex waves the photo album. "It's all in here. Photographic evidence. My dad loves *us*. You two are, like, I don't know—*actors*, and we're the real thing. I don't know why I ever thought differently. He's obviously with you for some other reason. Are you rich? Do you have money? Is that it?"

Sherry is still crouched, and Caleb, naked and shiny, reaches for her. She moves her body so that she's facing Alex, concealing her son.

"Alex, I think it would be best if you leave now," she said. "Okay? Can you go?"

"No, I can't *go*!" Alex yelled. "You can't just fucking dismiss me!"

"Okay. Okay." Sherry's voice is soft. Behind her, Caleb starts to wail. "Well, can I take Caleb to his room? He gets upset with loud noises. Can I do that, Alex? Get your brother settled into bed?"

"My brother?" Alex explodes. "My *brother*? I don't have a brother. This is just some kid, some kid my dad's going to leave one day, just like he left me and my mom. You see that, don't you? How easily he deserted us? He's going to do that to you one day, you'll see."

Sherry is breathing hard but trying not to show it. "Alex, I'm sorry for upsetting you. But if I—"

"Just SHUT UP! Just—"

"What the hell is going on?" Alex's father's voice booms behind him.

"Oh, Sebastian, thank God," Sherry says, starting to cry. She turns to scoop up Caleb, holding his slippery wet body against hers, instantly soaking her gray sweater.

She stands, and the sight of mother and son crying together makes Alex's father grab him by the arm and pull him out of the bathroom and against a wall, where he presses Alex flat.

"What did you do?" his father hisses. "What did you say to them?"

"The truth!" Alex says. "That's all I ever say, the truth! It's not my fault people can't handle it." Alex pushes his father back, and for a moment, he's sure his father is going to punch him. Instead, Sebastian grips him by the bicep and hauls him toward the front door.

"Get out," his father says. "Right this instant."

Alex glares into his dad's bright hazel eyes. He hurls the photo album across the room, where it knocks over a vase. The crash brings Sherry—without Caleb—back into the doorframe of the living room. She's holding a phone.

"Sebastian, do I need to call—"

"No," Alex's father says, pushing him out the door. "He's leaving."

Alex stares at the front door, shaking with anger and betrayal. As hard as he can, he strikes his fist against the wood before returning to his car.

CHAPTER 7

"Mrs. Magana, you're going to have to come in as soon as possible." Mr. Rodriguez's voice sounded firm on the other end of the phone.

Six weeks had passed since Alex's first visit to Dr. Coker, and three weeks since his last appointment. The family had gone to the first two therapy sessions with Dr. Burton, but their schedules were already so packed that they weren't able to make their visits the priority that they'd initially vowed. And then there'd been the fiasco at Sebastian's house. Jennifer knew what falling off the wagon felt like. She was positive Alex had stopped taking his meds, but he wouldn't admit it. She'd called Dr. Burton and was waiting for him to call back. When the phone rang, that was who she was expecting.

"Yes, Mr. Rodriguez. What's the problem?" Jennifer asked, standing up at her desk. She'd never heard from the vice principal of Alex's school before.

"Alex is in my office, pretty scraped up. It took two other teachers and me to pull him off the other student in the parking lot. Not an ideal start to the day." Jennifer could hear the frown in Mr. Rodriguez's voice, and her stomach sank. He was fatherly, and his disappointment stung.

"I'll be right there," she said quietly.

Through the glass in the vice principal's office, Jennifer saw Alex slumped against the sterile white wall, an ice pack over his left eye. His body was languid, draped over the side of the chair with his free hand hanging just a few inches off the floor. He looked as if he'd been through the wringer, but his expression was vacant.

"Mr. Rodriguez?" Jennifer said, stepping inside his office.

"Mrs. Magana, thank you for coming so quickly." Mr. Rodriguez motioned for her to take the empty seat next to her son. She slid into the seat, the vinyl sliding against her polyester dress slacks.

She turned to Alex. "What happened?" Her eyes were pleading. She crossed her fingers that her son would speak to her. Alex absently shook his head, continuing to stare at the wall. Jennifer turned to Mr. Rodriguez. "Sir, can you tell me what happened?"

Mr. Rodriguez smoothed his salt-and-pepper mustache as he leaned forward to prop his elbows on his desk. "Alex and another student got into a physical altercation in the parking lot. From several accounts, Alex started the fight with the other boy after the boy took a parking spot that Alex wanted. Alex got out of his car and used abusive language, and when the other student didn't back down, Alex took a swing at him. The student fought back, but when I was alerted to the situation, I found Alex on top of the other student, banging his head into the pavement. The other student was taken to the hospital by ambulance, and from what I've heard, the ER doctors have diagnosed him with a concussion, but he will be okay. Alex's use of force is completely unacceptable. Unfortunately, I've talked to the rest of our staff, and he will no longer be able to attend our school."

Mr. Rodriguez's words echoed into the hollow of Jennifer's heart. This school had been her last resort three years ago, and now they were turning her down, when Alex had only one year left.

"I understand," Jennifer said weakly. She swallowed the lump in her throat.

Alex followed Jennifer and slouched into the passenger seat. She kept sneaking glances at him as she drove; the buzz cut, though slightly grown out, still caught her off guard. It was like having a stranger in her car. How was she going to break this news to Sebastian, who was refusing to talk to Alex? How would she talk to Alex about being kicked out of school? She closed her eyes and exhaled at a red light.

"He deserved it," he said, barely above a murmur.

"Alex, don't say that. But what happened? Can you tell me?"

"Jonathan knew I was waiting for that spot. He saw me sitting with my turn signal on, but he cut around me and took it as soon as the other car pulled out. I put my car in park to talk to him, and then . . ." Alex trailed off. Jennifer could tell this was where his memory of the event got a little spotty. "Bettany was in his passenger seat. She hasn't been returning my messages, but she's in the car with *that* asshole." Alex's ears flushed.

"Oh, Alex," Jennifer said, as the light turned green. She had no idea who Bettany was. She was just pleased Alex was talking to her. She pulled the car into a gas station parking lot so she could unbuckle her seatbelt and embrace him.

In her arms, her son's tense shoulders relaxed and moved rhythmically as he devolved into sobs. Jennifer, unable to contain herself, cried along with him.

"Alex, I love you. I'm sure seeing Bettany with Jonathan was very hard. That makes sense. How you handled it, though, wasn't great. Jonathan had to go to the hospital. You could have . . ." Jennifer shuddered. "You could have hurt him very badly or even accidentally killed him."

"I wanted to, Mom," Alex said between sobs. "I wanted him to die." He buried his face further into Jennifer's shoulder, his tears coming so furiously that they puddled on her shirt in warm circles. "I'm fucking crazy, Mom. I'm broken."

Jennifer pushed Alex back so that she could look into his eyes. "You are not broken, Alex. This was just a bad day. We're going to figure this out. We're going to get there. It's going to take work, but just trust me. Okay?" she said.

Alex sniffed and nodded.

"Alex, you need to tell me the truth: Have you stopped taking your medication?"

Alex didn't answer.

Jennifer sighed. "Let's go home. Maybe you can take one of those 'as needed' pills the doctor gave us. That should help. While you're resting, I'll give Dr. Burton a call. Surely he'll have an idea of what to do next."

. . .

Dr. Burton made space for her that same afternoon. She would talk to him, one on one, and try to find something to help her son.

After explaining the day's events, she looked at Dr.

Burton and tossed her hands up in the air. "I know we should have continued coming to see you," she said tearfully. "I just . . . Everything seemed like it was going so well. Alex really seemed like he was getting better."

Dr. Burton nodded. "And he probably was. Unfortunately, medication adherence is a significant challenge for those living with bipolar disorder. They start feeling better, and suddenly the side effects that seemed minor before start to bother them. They start thinking maybe they don't need their medication anymore. Some people even stop on purpose because, even though they're glad to be rid of the lows, they miss the highs."

Jennifer nodded. She understood that Dr. Burton was trying to educate her, but this discussion just made her feel worse. She should have done something sooner, the minute she started seeing the signs: Alex's fast talking, his irritability, the drinking . . . She'd just been so desperate to believe things were getting better that she ignored her intuition.

"Well, the first step, of course, is to make sure he begins taking his medication again. But, Jennifer, you told me on the phone that he's been removed from his school. Have you decided what you're going to do next about his education?"

Jennifer shook her head. "The only option that I've thought of is to do the online school. Public school offers courses online, and he can still graduate on time. Of course, that opens a whole other can of worms regarding supervision at home while I'm at work."

"Have you discussed this with Alex's father yet?"

"I told him over the phone after Alex went to sleep. He's there at the house now, just in case, but we haven't had a chance to talk." Jennifer put her head down and massaged her temples. "Dr. Burton, I'm going to lose my job. They've been more than generous with me, but if Alex is at home all day . . . I just don't know what I'll do. I need to work!"

"I may have a solution for you, especially if you're thinking of homeschooling," Dr. Burton said. "Given the problems Alex is having, I think day treatment might be an option to explore. Our organization offers a day treatment program for kids and families. You'd have to talk to an intake counselor, but if Alex is accepted into the program, it lasts for up to eight weeks. He'd be assigned a social worker and evaluated by a child and adolescent psychiatrist. Alex would have a treatment plan and receive individual, group, and family therapy sessions."

Physicians may recommend a more intensive level of care than outpatient treatment if one is struggling with significant symptoms. The patient continues to reside at home but commutes to a treatment center up to seven days a week. Partial hospitalization focuses on the overall treatment of the individual, and is intended to avert or reduce inpatient hospitalization.

A physician may recommend inpatient hospitalization if the patient is struggling with significant symptoms and has either tried day treatment or day treatment is not available. The patient would be admitted into a psychiatric unit for intensive mental health treatment, including observation, diagnosis, individual and group therapy, and psychotropic medication management. The patient remains in the unit, including sleeping in the unit, until he or she is discharged. Inpatient hospitalization should be part of an overall plan of care—a coordinated effort between the individual, the family or other supporters, the inpatient treatment team, and outpatient service providers.

"What?" Jennifer asked. "He can be in intensive therapy all day?"

"He could come in the morning till noon. In the afternoons and evenings, he could complete his online coursework. If he makes good progress in therapy and the medication is also effective, this might be a good way to get him ready for senior year, maybe in his public high school," Dr. Burton said.

Jennifer sat, letting this new option sink in. She could work part time at the office and the rest of the time at home. She could get Alex the help he needed without having to leave her job.

"Dr. Burton, how do we get the ball rolling?"

* * *

Jennifer pulled her car into the garage and collected the paperwork that Dr. Burton had provided about the day treatment program. Everything was quiet when she opened the back door, and Jennifer held her breath until she found Sebastian at his laptop.

"Hey," he said, not looking up from the screen. "He's still asleep. I was doing some research, trying to find out what the school options are. What did Dr. Burton say?"

Jennifer dropped onto one of the living room chairs alongside the couch where Sebastian sat. "Well, he had what I think is a good idea and our best option. I actually talked to an intake counselor already, I was so confident that you would agree."

"Jen, seriously?" Sebastian asked, looking over at the folder that Jennifer opened on the computer desk. "You just made a major decision for our son without even talking to me?"

Jennifer snapped, "You don't get to pick and choose, Sebastian. Yesterday you refused to speak to Alex; today you want to be involved in decisions about his care. I did what I think is best. Besides, I just talked to the counselor; I didn't sign our son's life away. Now, do you want to hear about it or not?"

They glared at each other before Sebastian sighed. "Tell me."

"Dr. Burton's clinic organization also offers adolescent day treatment or partial hospitalization," Jennifer said. "Alex can go in each day for the next two months or so. He'll be evaluated by a psychiatrist, be assigned a social worker, and receive individual and group therapy with a psychotherapist. We will also participate in family sessions. He can do online school in the afternoon. You looked up the online school?"

> A *psychotherapist* is an individual with either a doctoral degree (Ph.D.) or a master's degree, who is licensed by the state and treats clients using psychotherapy, or "talk therapy."

Sebastian nodded, gesturing at his computer screen. "That's just what I was reading when you walked in." He pulled out the overview form and read through it. Jennifer, as always, was astounded by how quickly Sebastian could read fairly dense material. "This looks pretty good . . ."

"Let's talk about it with him as soon as he wakes up. It's a nonnegotiable, though. I'll need you to stand strong by me with this," Jennifer said.

Sebastian met her eyes and nodded. "Thank you, for seeing the problem and for trying so hard to make everything work. I'm sorry I didn't stand strong by you sooner."

Jennifer bit her lip. She didn't think she could say anything without her voice cracking, so she simply stood and walked out of the room.

. . .

The sleeping pill wore off before it should have, and when Alex heard his parents talking, he had to get out. Shoeless, his footfall was silent, and he snatched his dad's keys from where they hung in the front hallway, just where he always left them when he lived here.

The CRV is clean and smells of the Hawaiian Breeze air freshener stuck into one of the air vents, a far cry from the sour stench of Alex's own car (whose keys his mother confiscated yet again). He doesn't know where he's driving, until he remembers the money he stole from his dad's house. Desperately, he feels around in his pockets—yes! They haven't been washed yet. Twenty-three dollars, right here.

He speeds to Mel's Liquors and buys one normal-sized bottle of Old Crow and one smaller one, and then he drives out to the lake. His parents are talking about shipping him off! They want to send him away, to be rid of him. His mom tells him he's not crazy, he's not broken, but then she goes behind his back and does this! "Partial hospitalization," he says out loud, staring out at the water. It's started to thaw. You can see the waves moving beneath the ice.

Alex drinks quickly, drinks until both bottles are gone and he can't feel any part of his body. He wonders at this, how drinking can both make him feel and make him numb, and right now, that's what he wants. He wants to feel nothing. Not the pain of his brokenness, not the fear of his future, not the rage at his father, not the sadness of his mother, not even the deliciousness of Bettany or the thrill of the electricity he's come to love and hate. He wants to feel nothing. Nothing, nothing—

His head lolls back against the seat and then snaps forward again. The world is wild outside his windshield, kaleidoscopic and hard to pin down. He's confused. He wants to go home. He puts the car in drive and grips the wheel as tightly as he can, only letting go to cover one eye. He sees better with one eye. Not double. Only one-and-a-halfness.

It's dusk and the road and sky have faded into the same dull gray. Alex is weaving between lanes; he knows it but can't seem to keep himself in line. He wants to go home. That's what he wants. But he's starting to worry; he keeps dozing off, almost, a nauseous kind of sleepiness overtaking him. He's scared. He keeps one hand on the wheel while he fumbles for his phone on the console, squeezing one eye shut. He calls his mother, and when she answers, sounding panicked, he says, "Mom? Mom, I think I fucked up," and then he is consumed by headlights.

CHAPTER 8

There could be nothing more horrifying than hearing your son scream, listening to the obscene crash of metal on metal, utterly helpless. Jennifer had screamed too, a high-pitched keen she'd never heard herself make before. She was incoherent, sobbing, "He's dead, he's dead," as Sebastian called the police, demanding any information about car accidents nearby. The house line rang before Sebastian found what they needed, a police officer telling Jennifer which hospital Alex had been taken to. He was alive. The other car had swerved at the last moment, sideswiping the CRV and sending it rolling, but Alex was so drunk that his body was limp and pliant as clay. They were probably pumping his stomach now, the officer said.

Alex woke up in the middle of that night, wincing and unfocused. He didn't know where he was or what had happened. The last he remembered was drinking by the lake. No, he wasn't trying to kill himself, he said, but Jennifer just shook her head.

"They're going to put you in psychiatric hold for seventy-two hours," she said. She was so devastated that she could barely look at him.

"Psychiatric hold?" Alex protested. "You see? You do think I'm crazy!"

"Alejandro Magana, stop it right now," Jennifer said, her tone harsh. "You do not get to object. You do not get to complain. You nearly *killed* yourself! And other people, too."

At this, Alex looks stricken. "Did I—did I hurt anybody?"

Jennifer blinked. Her eyes stung. You've hurt *me*! she wanted to say. You've hurt your father. You've hurt your whole family. With great restraint, she said, "Yes. But they're going to be fine. Alex, there are going to be serious legal consequences."

Alex shut his eyes and let out a shuddering breath. "God, Mom. What's wrong with me?"

It took everything Jennifer had, all the love in her soul, to not shake him and shout, "Bipolar! You know that! This was all completely avoidable!" Instead, she said, "Alex. Your blood work came back. I know you've gone off your meds."

Alex made a snuffling noise, and it took Jennifer a moment to realize that he was crying through his broken nose. The sound was terrible. "I'm sorry," Alex gasped. "Mom, I'm so sorry. I don't know why—I don't know why I did it. At first it was an honest mistake. I just forgot. And then nothing happened, so I thought . . ."

"You thought you didn't need them," Jennifer completed, thinking about her talk with Dr. Burton.

Alex nodded. "But I do," he said, sounding unbearably heavy.

"Yes, honey. You do."

"Am I ever going to get better?" Alex stared pleadingly at Jennifer.

She reached out and ran her fingers through the rough growth of his hair. "You can," she said. "But this is a lifelong thing, Alex. You can get better if you do the work.

Do you understand that? Do you think you can do it?"

For a few minutes, all Alex could do was cry. Then he said, "I want to."

Jennifer leaned down and kissed him, resting her head lightly against his.

"Where's Dad?" Alex asked, almost inaudibly.

"He's been with me all day," Jennifer said. "He was exhausted. I told him I'd call him when you woke up."

Alex's dark eyes glinted with more tears. "Can you tell him I'm sorry?"

• • •

It had been a week since the accident, and they had an appointment to meet with Brian, the social worker at the day treatment program Dr. Burton had recommended. The mood in Jennifer's car was quiet and solemn. There just didn't seem to be much to say.

The three walked through the parking lot and into the lobby of the clinic. Jennifer and Sebastian instinctively walked on either side of Alex, whether to protect him or ensure he didn't bolt, Jennifer wasn't sure. The walls were a soothing, pale green. Sebastian led Alex over to have a seat while Jennifer checked the family in.

"Alex?" A young African-American man called them back after just a few moments. He was tall and strapping, with the build of a college athlete. "Hey, I'm Brian." The man shook Alex's hand, looking him straight in the eye. Alex returned the handshake robotically, but Brian's body language didn't change. "Are these your folks?" Brian asked, looking back to Sebastian and Jennifer.

Alex nodded briefly, and Brian shook both of their hands.

"If you'll follow me, we can sit and chat for a while," he said.

Jennifer felt at ease in Brian's presence. She appreciated the way that he addressed Alex first and them second. If Alex allowed himself, he might feel safe here.

Brian led the family back into a small office lined with bookshelves. He had a small desk with a laptop pressed against the wall, and Led Zeppelin and Carlos Santana peeked out from either side of his computer screen.

"You into Santana?" Alex asked. Jennifer and Sebastian exchanged glances, pleasantly surprised by Alex's interest.

"Yeah. I play a little guitar. What about you?" Brian asked, smiling.

"I used to play, but I stopped. My grandfather was an incredible musician. Dad has some early tapes of him. I never met him, but he was amazing," Alex said, quietly bragging.

"That's awesome, Alex!" Brian said, relaxing into the chair and motioning for the family to make themselves comfortable. "Let's see if we can bring in our instruments and rock out one day. While I'm your social worker, I also really dig music, so I sometimes like to play with the people who are here."

"Really?" Alex was disarmed. Jennifer could nearly read his mind—a place where he could play guitar with a guy who seemed pretty cool? Maybe this wasn't the straightjacket funny farm he'd imagined.

"Yeah. Do you want to hear about what else we do?" Brian asked.

"Sure," Alex said, suddenly aloof again.

"So we're a multimodal approach here. That means

it's not one-size-fits-all. Your treatment plan is *your* plan, with input from a board-certified child and adolescent psychiatrist—that's Dr. Nixon, whom you'll meet—as well as behavioral specialists; education specialists; experiential therapists, such as art and recreation therapists; dietitians; me; and most importantly, you and your parents. A lot of people looking out for you, buddy."

Alex nodded, and Jennifer felt a stab of hope, sweet and painful.

"Dr. Nixon will talk to you about your medication. I understand there have been some issues there. Then we'll go to group. Your group has seven people in it right now. Everyone is between fifteen and eighteen, and they've had pretty similar experiences as you. Patricia runs those sessions. She's awesome. Together, you guys will talk about where you've been and where you want to go. After that, you'll meet with me, and we'll have some time together, and then we all join up again and sometimes play some games, sometimes do some kind of cool art . . . We just work on projects, whatever interests you." Brian smiled again at Alex, who returned the smile.

"The coolest thing about here," Brian continued, "especially compared to school, is that there are lots of people around for you to talk to when you feel like you need it. One night a week, your parents come back with you, and you'll meet with Dr. Burton. You'll talk about ways to help everyone communicate better and hopefully have things go better at home," Brian said.

Alex nodded thoughtfully. "That doesn't sound too bad. Hey, Brian?" he said.

Brian smiled. "Yeah, man?"

"Do you—does everyone here know . . . about me?

About everything? Everything I've done?"

Brian said, "Everyone involved in your treatment plan is pretty informed, yeah," he said. "But Alex, no one is here to judge you or punish you. It might sound cliché, but this is a safe place. Okay?"

Alex stared at his lap and nodded.

"Cool. I want to show you around and get you set up with Dr. Nixon. Mr. and Mrs. Magana, if you guys will follow me to the waiting room, you can look this over while we're with Dr. Nixon." Brian handed Jennifer the same folder that she had brought home the day Dr. Burton told her of this program, and then led them all from the room.

When they were situated back in the waiting room, Sebastian looked over at his ex-wife. "It's like they . . ." He trailed off, unsure how to finish his own sentence.

"They seem to understand him," Jennifer said, relieved. She smiled at Sebastian, then looked down, engrossed by the detail with which the program was laid out before her. She couldn't believe that such a program existed and was heartbroken that her family had to fall so far before finding it.

An hour later, Brian returned.

"Mr. and Mrs. Magana," Brian said, "Dr. Nixon would like to talk to you now. Alex is still with her. Will you follow me?"

Jennifer nodded.

Brian led them down a hallway and then knocked lightly on an open door. A woman about Jennifer's age appeared around the desk. "Hi! I'm Dr. Nixon," she said, smoothing her dark hair behind her ears. "Please, have a seat." She motioned to the two empty chairs in front of her desk. Alex occupied the third.

"So, what do you think so far?" Jennifer asked Alex softly.

Alex shrugged, and Jennifer squeezed her son's shoulder.

Dr. Nixon pushed her wire-rimmed glasses further up her nose. "I wanted to talk with you briefly about Alex's medication. Unfortunately, it's not uncommon to try three, four medications before finding the medication and dosage that is effective. The one I'd like for us to try is another mood stabilizer—so, same classification as the first one, but hopefully with fewer of the side effects that became bothersome to Alex."

"Can you tell us more?" Jennifer asked. She wished Dr. Coker had mentioned the likelihood of needing to try different combinations.

"Similar to the first mood stabilizer you took, Alex, this will manage both manic and depressive symptoms. From the recent events and careful logging that you've done, Jennifer, we can see that Alex is cycling fairly rapidly without medication. Alex," she said, turning to him, "based on our conversation, it appears that you're currently showing more depressive symptoms. This is nothing you've done wrong; it's only a way that your brain is working differently. My hope is to get your thinking and emotions more balanced relatively soon, so that you can fully benefit from the resources that you'll have over the next few months. Make sense?" Dr. Nixon gave the entire family a sweeping glance.

"What kinds of side effects might there be, Dr. Nixon?" Jennifer asked.

"Perhaps some nausea, GI upset," Dr. Nixon said. "We won't know exactly how Alex will respond until we have him on it. However, starting this while he's here is the best bet, as I will be monitoring his blood work closely, and Alex will have the opportunity to talk to any number of people about any effects he's feeling."

> Some psychotropic medications require blood to be drawn at regular intervals to determine whether the blood level of the medication is at the therapeutic or appropriate range. Some medications that require these blood draws include lithium, Depakote, and Tegretol.

Sebastian asked, point-blank, "So you'll know if he stops taking it?"

Jennifer looked at Alex, expecting a reaction, but Alex just looked sad.

"Yes," Dr. Nixon said, "but our intention, Alex, is to help you understand the importance of adherence and give you some tools that might help if ever you're tempted to stop taking it again."

They all looked at Alex, who, despite the short hair and broken nose, suddenly looked very young.

"Okay," Alex said.

"Okay," Jennifer repeated.

Sebastian nodded. "Let's give it a shot."

CHAPTER 9

The first week of day treatment is whitewashed in Alex's memory. He was depressed then, floating from space to space with no motivation or sense of purpose. He remembers thinking he'd "do his time." Each aimless day was another day closer to not having to come anymore.

Then he supposed the new medication Dr. Nixon had prescribed started to kick in. The quiet despair, the nihilistic wondering of what the point was to all this, lifted enough for him to contribute in a group session. It was a social skills group, and the group leader, Patricia, asked them to consider a social situation that had gone badly for them recently. Hot with shame, Alex remembered how he'd yelled at Sherry. The memory was murky, but he couldn't erase the image of her holding the soaked baby, crying in relief that Alex's dad was home. She'd been afraid. She'd been afraid of *him*. When he thought back, he wondered how much worse the situation might have gotten if his dad hadn't shown up right then. He wondered whether he could have hurt Sherry or even the baby, and he was so lost in this sad revisiting that he didn't realize Patricia was calling his name.

"Alex?" she said again, softly. She smiled at him. "Is there anything you'd like to share?"

Alex opened his mouth to say no, but instead the whole story, what he remembered of it, came burbling out. His fists were clenched on his lap, his face and arm-pits sweating. When he looked up, he expected to see dis-gust on everyone's faces. He was surprised that a couple of the kids were nodding, and Patricia's pale-moon face was open and warm.

"Thank you, Alex. Why don't we explore this a bit more with some role playing?" A few of the kids groaned, and Patricia laughed. "I know, I know, it's not everyone's fa-vorite, but trust me—it's really beneficial."

Patricia asked them to pair up, and Alex found him-self facing Ashley, a red-haired girl who also had bipolar I.

"So Alex shared a situation that didn't go too well," Patricia said. "One that ended with a pretty negative re-action. I'd like for you all to think of a situation like this. Do you have one in mind?"

Enough people in the room nodded for Patricia to continue. "Great. Now—can you think of other ways you could have handled it? Two or three different choices you could have made to improve the outcome?"

Alex said, "But the thing is, I don't think I could have."

"What do you mean?" Patricia asked.

"When I'm like that—you know, manic—it's like I'm a whole other person. And what I'm doing makes sense at the time. So it's not like I could've stopped myself or done something different, because I thought what I was doing was right."

Patricia nodded. "That's a keen insight, Alex. But what about now? What are some things you could say to Sherry now to create a better outcome?"

Alex frowned. It hadn't occurred to him that he could

97

make a better outcome; he'd thought what's done is done.

Patricia said, "Think about that for a moment. Ashley, I'd like for you to play Sherry. Then you guys will switch so that Ashley can work through her situation."

Patricia made her way around the room, quietly helping people who were struggling. Alex scuffed his Converse on the tile. He looked up at Ashley.

"This is so weird," he said.

She laughed. "Yeah. But come on. I'm Sherry."

Alex sighed. He mumbled, "I'm sorry I scared you, Sherry. I was just so mad."

Uncertainly, Ashley said, "Why were you mad?"

"Because you ruined my family!" The words were out of Alex's mouth before he could stop them.

Patricia overheard and stepped closer. "Alex, your anger makes complete sense. But do you think maybe there's a way of explaining it in a less attacking way so that Sherry can really *hear* it?"

Alex let out a long breath, almost a huff. "Fine. I was mad because—because we lost my dad. And I blamed you for that."

Patricia nodded. "Good."

"But I shouldn't have treated you that way," Alex continued. "I shouldn't have scared you and Caleb like that. It was wrong and I'm sorry."

His apology to the fake Sherry brought surprised tears to his eyes. He cleared his throat, embarrassed.

"That's great work, Alex," Patricia said, smiling. She patted him on the shoulder. "How did that feel?"

"Weird. Good, I guess." Alex paused. "But what if Sherry doesn't want to see me and so I can't apologize?"

"Maybe you could think about writing her a letter?"

Patricia suggested.

The idea seemed ludicrous at first, and he almost made fun of it, but he didn't. A letter. He could actually do that. He could write her a letter. "Yeah," he said. "I guess that's a possibility."

"Good!" Patricia said. "Great job, you two. Why don't you go ahead and switch roles?"

For the rest of the session, they took turns improving on their past, rewriting history to lessen shame, guilt, anger, sadness. They apologized, cried, asked each other on dates, explained their emotions using "I language." After a while, Alex forgot about the awkwardness of pretending a stranger was his father's wife, or pretending to be a father himself. He got into it, and he started to realize that every situation held a multitude of possibilities, and that he had some control over which one of those possibilities played out. He felt—not powerful, not the way he did when he was manic, but something like *em*powered. He hoped he could hang on to it.

Now, six weeks in, Alex has a mantra: I can choose. The times he yearns nostalgically for just a sip of Old Crow, he thinks, I can choose. The time when—in the car, just the two of them—his father asked whether Alex could forgive him for the pain he'd caused, Alex thought, I can choose. He said, "I'll try." The time in family therapy when he yelled at his mom for saying, as she did frequently, "Alex, don't say that!" he reminded himself, I can choose, and he apologized. Then, so did his mother. She told him that he had a right to his own feelings, and she shouldn't try to limit him because they made her afraid or uncomfortable. She wanted him to feel safe, she said. I can choose, Alex thought. So he said, "I do."

...

As the weather warmed, Jennifer found herself, ever so tentatively, relaxing. Six weeks into Alex's program and seven since the worst night of her life, she was feeling cautiously optimistic. Alex was taking his meds, and aside from some mild stomach upset, didn't seem to be experiencing any side effects. She was aware that that could change—that everything could change, once again, throwing her family into crisis—but for now, Alex was . . . better. He was running again, he didn't put up a struggle before day treatment in the morning, and his mood usually seemed good when Jennifer picked him up midday. In the afternoons, he sat at the computer and seemed able to focus on the public school's online coursework. He didn't gripe about not having access to his car, and it had been weeks since Jennifer had smelled alcohol on him. There was, as Dr. Coker had said during their first visit, reason to hope. But Jennifer didn't think she could ever get too comfortable; all it would take was a week off his meds for catastrophe to strike again. They lived on a knife-edge of normalcy. But for now, that was enough, and she was grateful.

HOW THESE BOOKS WERE CREATED

The ORP Library of disabilities books is the result of heart-felt collaboration between numerous people: the staff of ORP, including the CEO, executive director, psychologists, clinical coordinators, teachers, and more; the families of children with disabilities served by ORP, including some of the children themselves; and the Round Table Companies (RTC) storytelling team. To create these books, RTC conducted dozens of intensive, intimate interviews over a period of months and performed independent research in order to truthfully and accurately depict the lives of these families. We are grateful to all those who donated their time in support of this message, generously sharing their experience, wisdom, and—most importantly—their stories so that the books will ring true. While each story is fictional and not based on any one family or child, we could not have envisioned the world through their eyes without the access we were so lovingly given. It is our hope that in reading this uniquely personal book, you felt the spirit of everyone who contributed to its creation.

ACKNOWLEDGMENTS

Writing this book would not have been possible without the wisdom, patience, and experience of many generous individuals. In particular, the authors would like to thank Karen Johnson, retired Genesee Lake School health services director; Christy Lynch, Genesee Lake School therapist; Debbie Frisk, vice president at Oconomowoc Residential Programs, for her insights into day treatment programs; and Lorri Nelson, for facilitating interviews, organizing material, and generally helping to wrangle the many moving parts that go into writing a book. We would also like to thank the families who shared their journey with bipolar disorder and psychotropic medications with us in such candid detail. This group of people was invaluable in bringing Alex's story to life, and the authors are deeply grateful.

JEFFREY D. KRUKAR, PH.D.

BIOGRAPHY

Jeffrey Krukar, Ph.D., is a licensed psychologist and certified school psychologist with more than 20 years of experience working with children and families in a variety of settings, including community-based group homes, vocational rehabilitation services, residential treatment, juvenile corrections, public schools, and private practice. He earned his Ph.D. in educational psychology, with a school psychology specialization and psychology minor, from the University of Wisconsin-Milwaukee. Dr. Krukar is a Think:Kids Certified Trainer in Collaborative Problem Solving, and an assistant professor at the Wisconsin School of Professional Psychology. He is a registrant of the National Register of Health Service Providers in Psychology, and is also a member of the American Psychological Association.

As the psychologist at Genesee Lake School in Oconomowoc, WI, Dr. Krukar believes it truly takes a village to raise a child—to strengthen developmental foundations in relating, communicating, and thinking—so they can successfully return to their families and communities. Dr. Krukar hopes the ORP Library of disabilities books will bring to light the stories of children and families to a world that is generally not aware of their challenges and successes, as well as offer a sense of hope to those currently on this journey.

KATIE GUTIERREZ

BIOGRAPHY

Katie Gutierrez believes that a well-told story can transcend what a reader "knows" to be real about the world—and thus change the world for that reader. In every form, story is transformative, and Katie is proud to spend her days immersed in it as executive editor for Round Table Companies, Inc.

Since 2007, Katie has edited approximately 50 books and co-written several of the ORP Library of disabilities books, including *Meltdown* and *An Unlikely Trust*. She has been humbled by the stories she has heard and hopes these books will help guide families on their often-lonely journeys, connecting them with resources and support. She also hopes they will give the general population a glimpse into the Herculean jobs taken on so fiercely by parents, doctors, therapists, educators, and others who live with, work with, and love children like Alex.

Katie holds a BA in English and philosophy from Southwestern University and an MFA in fiction from Texas State University. She has contributed to or been profiled in publications including *Forbes*, *Entrepreneur* magazine, *People* magazine, *Hispanic Executive Quarterly*, and *Narrative* magazine. She can't believe she's lucky enough to do what she loves every day.

NICOLETTE E. WEISENSEL, M.D., F.A.P.A.

BIOGRAPHY

Nicolette E. Weisensel, M.D., F.A.P.A., is a board-certified psychiatrist who has experience in a variety of practice settings including outpatient, inpatient, residential, and day treatment. She has expertise in the treatment of eating disorders and Prader-Willi Syndrome. Dr. Weisensel earned her M.D. from the University of Wisconsin School of Medicine and Public Health. She also completed her psychiatry residency at the University of Wisconsin, serving as chief resident during her final year. She has presented at regional, national, and international conferences regarding eating disorders and Prader-Willi Syndrome. She is a member and fellow of the American Psychiatric Association.

JAMES G. BALESTRIERI

BIOGRAPHY

James G. Balestrieri is currently the CEO of Oconomowoc Residential Programs, Inc. (ORP). He has worked in the human services field for over 40 years, holding positions that run the gamut to include assistant maintenance, assistant cook, direct care worker, teacher's aide, summer camp counselor, bookkeeper, business administrator, marketing director, CFO, and CEO. Jim graduated from Marquette University with a B.S. in Business Administration (1977) and a Master's in Business Administration with an emphasis in Marketing (1988). He is also a Certified Public Accountant (Wisconsin—1982). Jim has a passion for creatively addressing the needs of those with impairments by managing the inherent stress among funding, programming, and profitability. He believes that those with a disability enjoy rights and protections that were created by the hard-fought efforts of those who came before them; that the Civil Rights movement is not just for minority groups; and that people with disabilities have a right to find their place in the world and to achieve their maximum potential as individuals. For more information, see *www.orp.com.*

ABOUT ORP

Oconomowoc Residential Programs, Inc. is an employee-owned family of companies making a difference in the lives of people with disabilities. With service locations throughout Wisconsin and Indiana, our dedicated staff of 2,400 people provides quality services and professional care to more than 1,950 children, adolescents, and adults with special needs. ORP provides a comprehensive continuum of care. Child and adolescent programs include developmentally appropriate education and treatment in settings specifically attuned to their needs. These include residential therapeutic education and vocational services for students from all around the country. For those in or near Wisconsin and Indiana, we offer community-based residential supports, in-home supports, in- and out-of-home respite care, and alternative therapeutic day-school programs. We provide special programs for students with specific academic and social issues relative to a wide range of complex disabilities, including autism spectrum disorders, Asperger's disorder, cognitive and developmental disabilities, anxiety disorders, depression, bipolar disorder, reactive attachment disorder, attention deficit disorder, severe emotional and behavioral issues, Prader-Willi Syndrome, and other impairments. Our adult services continuum includes community-based residential services for people with intellectual, developmental, and physical disabilities, brain injury, mental health and other behavioral impairments, and the medically fragile.

We also provide independent living homes, supervised apartments, community-based supports for adults in mental health crisis, day service programs, and respite services.

At ORP, our guiding principle is passion: a passion for the people we serve and for the work we do.

For a comprehensive look at each of our programs, please visit *www.orp.com*. For a collection of resources for parents, educators and administrators, and health-care professionals who are raising or supporting children with disabilities, please visit the ORP Library at *www.orplibrary.com*.

RESOURCES FOR FAMILIES, LOVED ONES, AND PROFESSIONALS

American Academy of Child and Adolescent Psychiatry
www.aacap.org

American Psychiatric Association
www.psychiatry.org

Mayo Clinic
www.mayoclinic.org

National Alliance on Mental Illness (NAMI)
www.nami.org

National Institute of Mental Health
www.nimh.nih.gov

Understanding Mental Disorders: Your Guide to DSM-5

University of Wisconsin Hospital and Clinics
www.uwhealth.org

PSYCHOTROPIC MEDICATIONS

Finding Balance is the first of three books in the ORP Library focusing on the use of psychotropic medication in children and adolescents. Based on dozens of interviews with parents and clinicians, the book tells the fictional (but all too real) story of Alex, a seventeen-year-old diagnosed with bipolar disorder. From exploring challenges with side effects, adherence, and dosage and medication changes, to highlighting successes, to explaining the importance of a comprehensive biopsychosocial treatment plan, the medication book series aims to educate families, caregivers, and healthcare professionals on the short-term and long-term impact of including psychotropic medications in a child's treatment plan.

FINDING BALANCE

A FAMILY'S JOURNEY TO TREATMENT
FOR BIPOLAR DISORDER

*Look for additional books on children and
psychotropic medications coming soon!*

ASPERGER'S DISORDER

Meltdown and its companion comic book, *Melting Down*, are both based on the fictional story of Benjamin, a boy diagnosed with Asperger's disorder and additional challenging behavior. From the time Benjamin is a toddler, he and his parents know he is different: he doesn't play with his sister, refuses to make eye contact, and doesn't communicate well with others. And his tantrums are not like normal tantrums; they're meltdowns that will eventually make regular schooling—and day-to-day life—impossible. Both the prose book, intended for parents, educators, and mental health professionals, and the comic for the kids themselves demonstrate that the journey toward hope isn't simple . . . but with the right tools and teammates, it's possible.

MELTDOWN

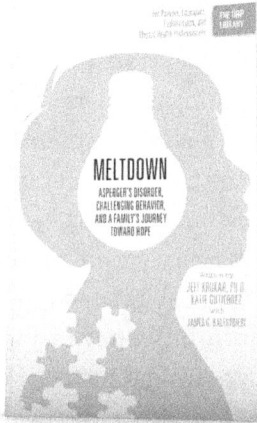

ASPERGER'S DISORDER, CHALLENGING BEHAVIOR, AND A FAMILY'S JOURNEY TOWARD HOPE

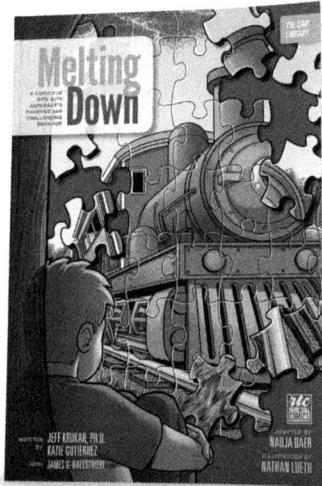

MELTING DOWN

A COMIC FOR KIDS WITH ASPERGER'S DISORDER AND CHALLENGING BEHAVIOR

AUTISM SPECTRUM DISORDER

Mr. Incredible shares the fictional story of Adam, a boy diagnosed with autistic disorder. On Adam's first birthday, his mother recognizes that something is different about him: he recoils from the touch of his family, preferring to accept physical contact only in the cool water of the family's pool. As Adam grows older, he avoids eye contact, is largely nonverbal, and has very specific ways of getting through the day; when those habits are disrupted, intense meltdowns and self-harmful behavior follow. From seeking a diagnosis to advocating for special education services, from keeping Adam safe to discovering his strengths, his family becomes his biggest champion. The journey to realizing Adam's potential isn't easy, but with hope, love, and the right tools and teammates, they find that Adam truly is *Mr. Incredible*. The companion comic in this series, inspired by social stories, offers an innovative, dynamic way to guide children—and parents, educators, and caregivers—through some of the daily struggles experienced by those with autism.

MR. INCREDIBLE

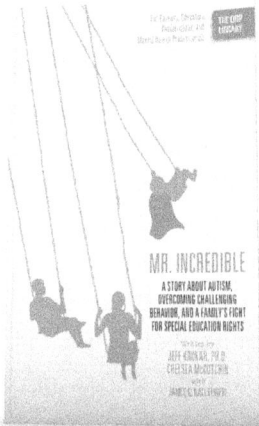

A STORY ABOUT AUTISM,
OVERCOMING CHALLENGING
BEHAVIOR, AND A FAMILY'S FIGHT
FOR SPECIAL EDUCATION RIGHTS

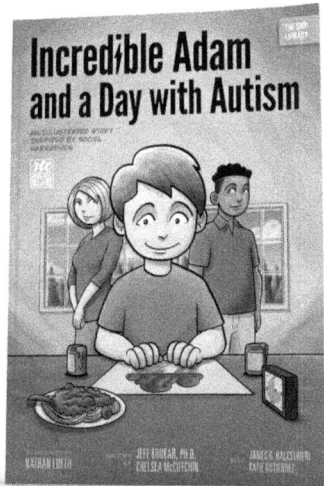

INCREDIBLE ADAM
AND A DAY WITH AUTISM

AN ILLUSTRATED STORY
INSPIRED BY SOCIAL NARRATIVES

BULLYING

Nearly one third of all school children face physical, verbal, social, or cyber bullying on a regular basis. Educators and parents search for ways to end bullying, but as that behavior becomes more sophisticated, it's harder to recognize and stop. In *Classroom Heroes*, Jason is a quiet, socially awkward seventh grader who has long suffered bullying in silence. His parents notice him becoming angrier and more withdrawn, but they don't realize the scope of the problem until one bully takes it too far—and one teacher acts on her determination to stop it. Both *Classroom Heroes* and *How to Be a Hero*—along with a supporting coloring book (*Heroes in the Classroom*) and curriculum guide (*Those Who Bully and Those Who Are Bullied*)—recognize that stopping bullying requires a change in mindset: adults and children must create a community that simply does not tolerate bullying. These books provide practical yet very effective strategies to end bullying, one student at a time.

CLASSROOM HEROES

ONE CHILD'S STRUGGLE
WITH BULLYING AND
A TEACHER'S MISSION
TO CHANGE SCHOOL
CULTURE

HOW TO
BE A HERO

A COMIC BOOK
ABOUT BULLYING

HEROES IN THE
CLASSROOM

AN ACTIVITY BOOK
ABOUT BULLYING

THOSE WHO BULLY
AND THOSE WHO
ARE BULLLIED

A GUIDE FOR
CREATING HEROES IN
THE CLASSROOM

FAMILY SUPPORT

Schuyler Walker was just four years old when he was diagnosed with autism, bipolar disorder, and ADHD. In 2004, childhood mental illness was rarely talked about or understood. With knowledge and resources scarce, Schuyler's mom, Christine, navigated a lonely maze to determine what treatments, medications, and therapies could benefit her son. In the years since his diagnosis, Christine has often wished she had a "how to" guide that would provide the real mom-to-mom information she needed to survive the day and, in the end, help her family navigate the maze with knowledge, humor, grace, and love. Christine may not have had a manual at the beginning of her journey, but she hopes this book will serve as yours.

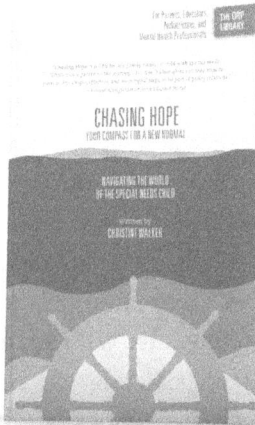

CHASING HOPE
YOUR COMPASS FOR A NEW NORMAL
NAVIGATING THE WORLD
OF THE SPECIAL NEEDS CHILD

PRADER-WILLI SYNDROME

Estimated to occur once in every 15,000 births, Prader-Willi Syndrome is a rare genetic disorder that includes features of cognitive disabilities, problem behaviors, and, most pervasively, chronic hunger that leads to dangerous overeating and its life-threatening consequences. *Insatiable: A Prader-Willi Story* and its companion comic book, *Ultra-Violet: One Girl's Prader-Willi Story*, draw on dozens of intensive interviews to offer insight into the world of those struggling with Prader-Willi Syndrome. Both books tell the fictional story of Violet, a vivacious young girl born with the disorder, and her family, who—with the help of experts—will not give up their quest to give her a healthy and happy life.

INSATIABLE

A PRADER-WILLI STORY

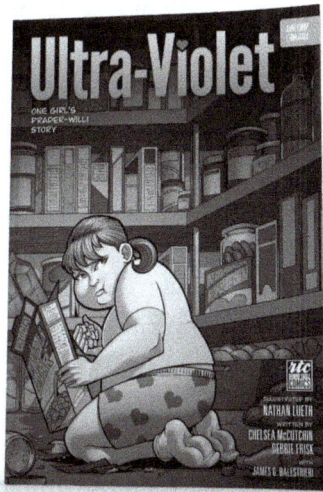

ULTRA-VIOLET

ONE GIRL'S PRADER-WILLI STORY

REACTIVE ATTACHMENT DISORDER

Loving Harder, *An Unlikely Trust*, and *Alina's Story* share the journeys of children diagnosed with reactive attachment disorder. *Loving Harder* is the true story of the Hetzel family, while *An Unlikely Trust* is a composite story based on dozens of intensive interviews with parents and clinicians. *Alina's Story* is a companion children's book and valuable therapeutic tool, offering a beautiful and accessible way for children with RAD to understand their own stories. The families in these books know their adopted children need help and work endlessly to find it, eventually discovering a special school that will teach the children new skills. Slowly, the children get better at expressing their feelings and solving problems. For the first time in their lives, they realize they are safe and loved . . . and capable of loving in return.

AN UNLIKELY TRUST

ALINA'S STORY OF ADOPTION, COMPLEX TRAUMA, HEALING, AND HOPE

ALINA'S STORY

LEARNING HOW TO TRUST, HEAL, AND HOPE

LOVING HARDER

OUR FAMILY'S ODYSSEY THROUGH ADOPTION AND REACTIVE ATTACHMENT DISORDER

www.ingramcontent.com/pod-product-compliance
Lightning Source LLC
LaVergne TN
LVHW051128080426
835510LV00018B/2291